ALONG THE SEASHORE

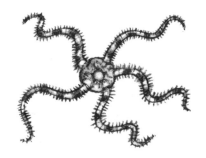

Books by Margaret Waring Buck

ALONG THE SEASHORE

Written and illustrated by

MARGARET WARING BUCK

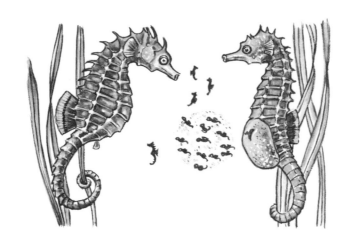

Nashville   ABINGDON PRESS   *New York*

FOR CAROL AND DONNIE,
and other girls and boys
who like to explore along the seashore.

THIS BOOK is for beginning naturalists to help in their understanding of marine life. It describes many of the plants and animals to be found along the Atlantic, Pacific, and Gulf coasts of the United States. Some of the northern species will also be found along the Canadian and Alaskan coasts. Some of the southern species are also seen along the Mexican coast. The life history of each kind of animal is given and a description of some of the commoner species. The manuscript of the book was read and checked for accuracy by specialists in the biological sciences.

The author wishes to express her thanks and appreciation to John S. Rankin, Jr., Director, Marine Biological Laboratory, University of Connecticut; William Niering, Associate Professor, Department of Botany, Connecticut College; Duryea Morton, Director, Audubon Center, Greenwich, Connecticut; Charles Baxter, Instructor, Department of Biological Sciences, Stanford University; Charles Alex Shivers, Research Fellow, Department of Biological Sciences, Florida State University.

CONTENTS

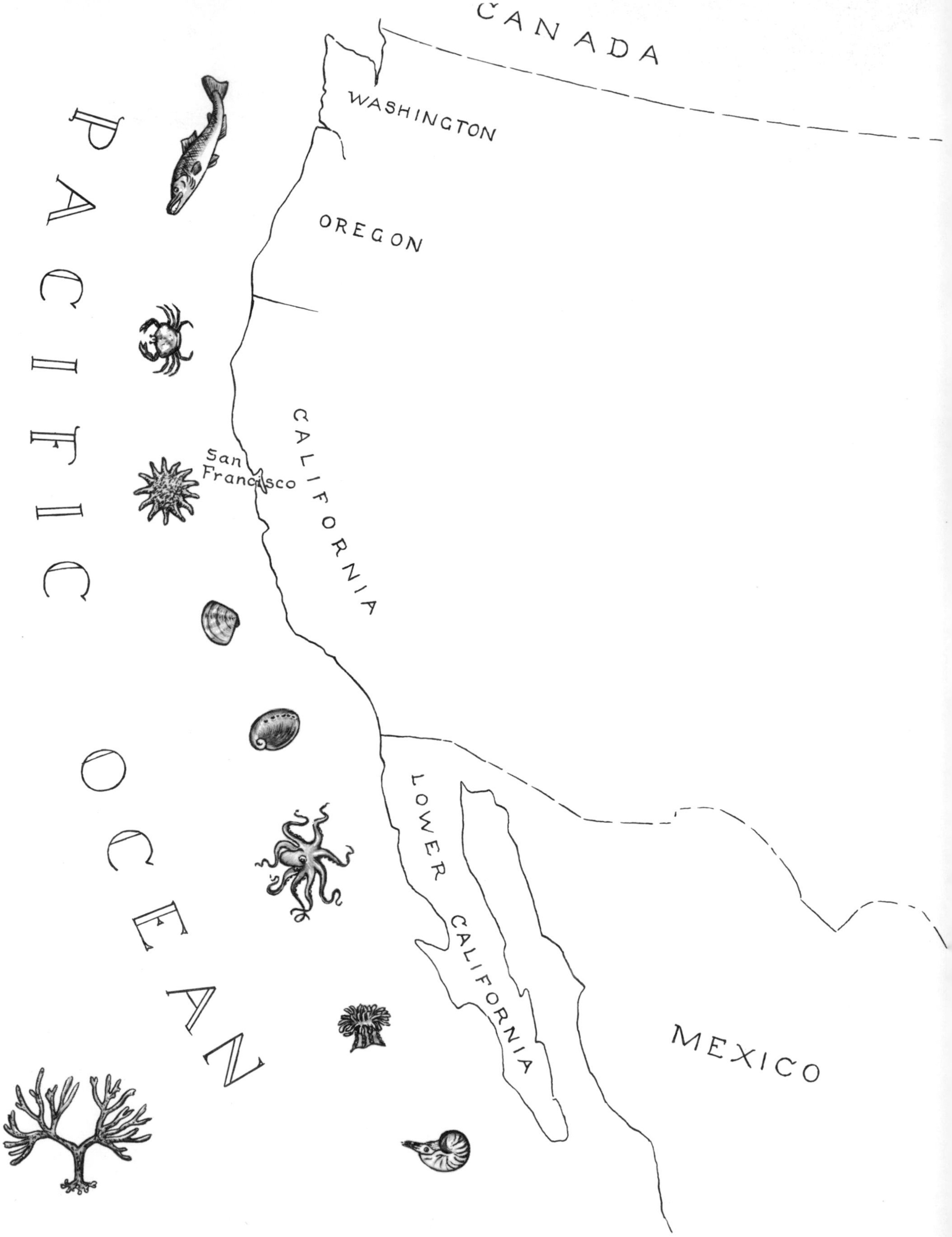

PACIFIC OCEAN

CANADA

WASHINGTON

OREGON

CALIFORNIA

San Francisco

LOWER CALIFORNIA

MEXICO

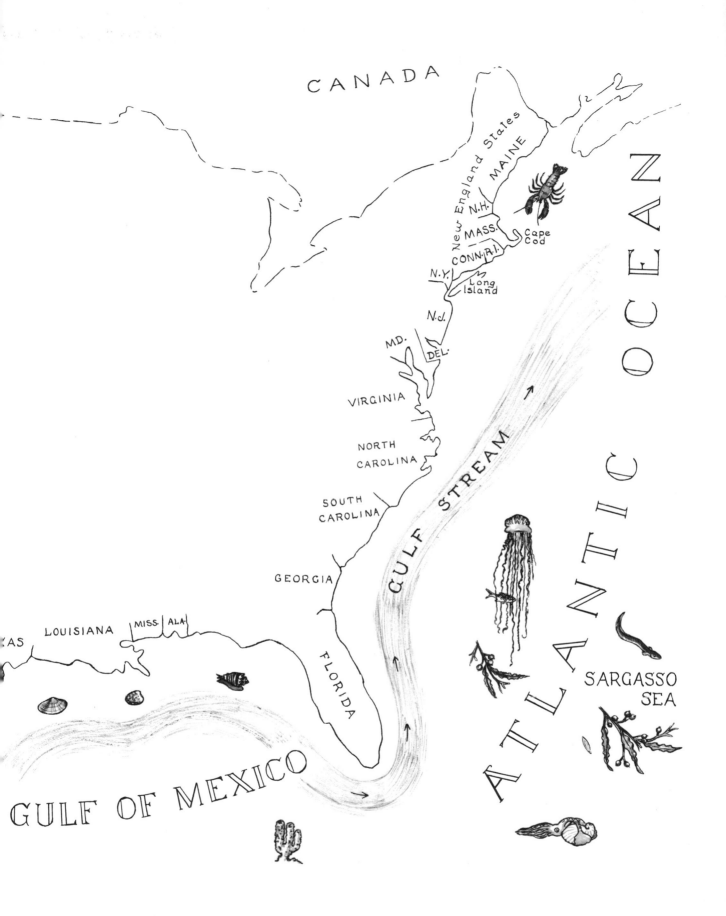

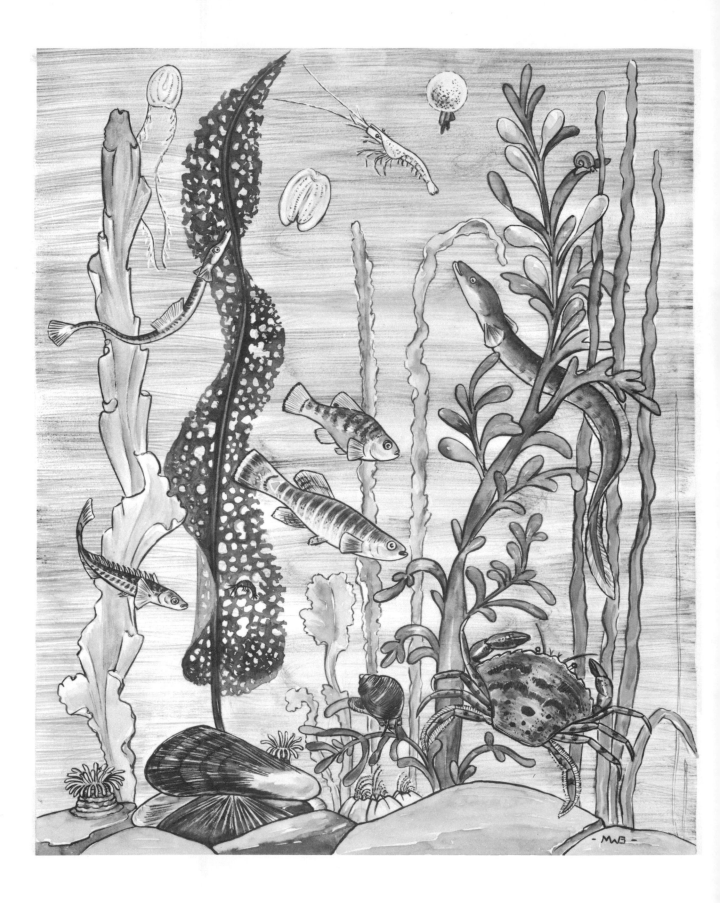

This book begins with plants that grow beside the sea and plants (algae) that grow in the sea. It continues with animal life of the sea starting with simple forms such as sponges and continuing with more complex groups. It concludes with the higher forms of animal life—the fishes and the water birds.

SEASIDE PLANTS: GRASSES

Many different kinds of grasslike plants grow in tidal marshes and in the sand along all of our coasts.

SEA OATS grow to a height of 3 or 4 feet in sand along the southern Atlantic and Gulf coasts. They bear clusters of small, flat, seedlike fruits.

BEACH GRASS grows on dunes and sandy shores along the Atlantic coast, and it has been planted on the Pacific coast because it is useful as a sand binder. It has stiff blades and erect fruiting spikes.

The SHORE RUSH, found in brackish water along the Atlantic coast, has a cluster of small fruits. The SEASIDE RUSH of the northeast has larger bur-like fruits. Both kinds of rushes have triangular stems.

SANDBUR is a sprawling grass that grows in sand along all of our shores and inland. Its clusters of burs have sharp spines that prick and cling.

CORD GRASSES grow in salt marshes along both coasts, where they serve as mud binders. They have long, tough, tapering blades, cordlike when dry. The fruiting parts are clusters of flattened spikelets at the top of a stiff stem.

REEDS are found in wet places throughout our country. The feathery fruiting heads on stems to 12 feet high are a common sight in marshes. The plants spread by means of running rootstalks.

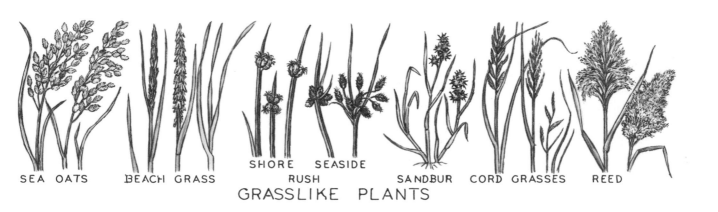

SEA OATS   BEACH GRASS   SHORE   SEASIDE   SANDBUR   CORD GRASSES   REED
                            RUSH
GRASSLIKE PLANTS

SEA LAVENDER   ROSE MALLOW   MARSH MALLOW   SEASIDE ASTER   SEASIDE GOLDENROD

FLOWERS: EAST COAST

FLOWERS: EAST COAST

SEA LAVENDER grows in salt marshes along the Atlantic and Gulf coasts. The leathery, oblong leaves are in a cluster close to the ground. In summer the flower stem, 1 or 2 feet high, has single rows of tiny lavender flowers along its top branches.

The ROSE MALLOW or SEA HOLLYHOCK has stalks that grow from 4 to 7 feet high in brackish marshes along the Atlantic coast. The large pink or white flowers, similar to those of the hollyhock, appear at the top of the stalks in late summer.

The MARSH MALLOW grows from 2 to 4 feet high in salt marshes along our northeastern coast. The pink flowers bloom in small clusters in summer. The root is used in making candy.

The SEASIDE ASTER grows 1 or 2 feet high in sandy soil along the northeastern coast. The stiff stems have oblong leaves and there are longer, thicker leaves near the ground. The flowers, purple with orange centers, bloom in late summer and fall.

SEASIDE GOLDENROD grows in sandy soil and salt marshes to a height of 4 feet. It has a stout stem and leathery, dark green leaves. Showy clusters of small golden flowers bloom in late summer and fall.

FLOWERS: WEST COAST

SAND VERBENAS grow on beaches. They have sprawling stems and, in spring and summer, clusters of small, fragrant flowers. A yellow variety is found all along the coast; a pink variety grows in California.

The SEA FIG grows in sandy places in California. Its thick, three-sided leaves are pale blue-green with reddish tips. In spring it has purple-pink flowers 2 or 3 inches across. The fruit is figlike and edible.

The ICE PLANT has flat, light blue-green or reddish leaves encrusted with tiny beadlike swellings filled with fluid. In spring it has white or pinkish flowers about 1 inch across. These plants form glistening carpets in dry places in California.

The BEACH PRIMROSE grows along the California coast, where it blooms throughout the year. It has pale grayish, downy leaves on leaning stems and yellow flowers about 1½ inches across.

The YELLOW TIDY-TIPS grows in sandy soil in California. It has pale green, deeply cut leaves on hairy, reddish stems about a foot high. The flowers, which bloom in spring, are yellow with white tips and are about 2 inches across.

Pink   Yellow
SAND VERBENAS   SEA FIG   ICE PLANT   BEACH PRIMROSE   TIDY-TIPS

FLOWERS: WEST COAST

GLASSWORT　　BEACH PEA　　MORNING GLORY　BINDWEED　　　　LUPINES

FLOWERS: BOTH COASTS

GLASSWORT or SAMPHIRE covers large areas in salt marshes along both of our coasts. Its fleshy, jointed stems, from 6 inches to 2 feet high, are light green in summer and red in fall. Its leaves and flowers are almost too small to see without a magnifying glass.

The BEACH PEA grows on a stout, sprawling stem in sand along both coasts. Its divided leaf has a tendril at the tip. In spring and summer it has clusters of large purple pealike flowers.

Wild morning glory vines are found near both coasts. The BEACH MORNING GLORY grows in sand along the western coast. It has thick, shiny green leaves that are broader than they are long and pink or purple flowers. HEDGE BINDWEED grows in waste places along the eastern coast and inland. It has triangular or arrow-shaped leaves, and its flowers are pink with white stripes.

LUPINES grow to a height of 2 feet or more in sandy soil near the coast and inland. They have spikes of pea-shaped flowers in early summer. The eastern kind has blue flowers. The western kinds have blue, pink, white, or yellow flowers.

SHRUBS

The MANZANITA is a handsome shrub, 3 or 4 feet high, that grows in the coastal hills of California. Its leaves are glossy green on the upper side, white and downy underneath. In spring it has clusters of small pink waxy flowers. The small greenish or rosy fruits that follow are edible.

BAYBERRY grows in sandy soil along the Atlantic coast. In summer it has greenish berries that later turn gray and last through the winter. The berries furnish a fragrant wax used for making candles.

BEACH PLUM grows in sandy soil along our northeastern coast. In spring it has white blossoms. In late summer it has small plums that are used to make jam or jelly.

YAUPON is a kind of holly that grows on sand dunes along the southeastern and Gulf coasts. It has clusters of small white flowers that are followed by red berries. The shiny, oval leaves are evergreen.

SEA GRAPE is a shrub or small tree that grows along the southern Florida shore. Its large leathery leaves are green with a reddish tinge. The clusters of small reddish berries look like grapes. They can be made into jelly.

MANZANITA　　　BAYBERRY　　　BEACH PLUM　　　YAUPON　　　SEA GRAPE

SHRUBS

GULF WEED

BROWN ALGAE

NODULOSE ROCKWEED

Bladders

BLADDER WRACK

Fruiting parts

SEAWEEDS: ALGAE

Seaweeds are algae. They have simple stalks and branches, blades in place of leaves, holdfasts instead of roots. They do not have flowers or seeds. The fruiting parts of the plant are in thickenings of the branches or blades. The plants also increase when pieces break off and grow. There are the blue-green, green, red, and brown groups of sea algae.

BROWN ALGAE

In this group are some of the largest and most interesting of the seaweeds.

GULF WEED or SARGASSUM looks like a vine with brown or greenish-brown berries and leaves. The leaves are narrow blades growing along the slender stalk and the berries are round air bladders. The stalk may be 3 feet or longer. Many species live in the warmer waters of the Atlantic, but some can be found further north. Related species are found in the Pacific.

ROCKWEEDS grow on rocks between tide levels on cool shores. The NODULOSE ROCKWEED of the Atlantic grows in sheltered places. It has dark brown stalks like twisted ribbons with short blades all along them and light brown egg-shaped air-filled bladders. The stalks grow several feet long. The BLADDER

WRACK lives in open surf or in bays along both coasts. It has flat stalks with a rib down the center. Some of the forked branches have pairs of gelatin-filled bladders. These seaweeds have male or female fruiting parts on the swollen ends of their branches. The reproducing cells float from these into the water and grow into new plants.

Many kinds of KELP are found in cool, deep water along both of our coasts. The FAN KELP of both coasts has a long single blade or a divided blade, like a palm leaf, on a stout stalk that may be 5 feet long. The RIBBON KELP of the Pacific has slender, ribbon-like blades. They rise in a bunch from a globular float on a flexible stalk that may be 100 feet long. The GIANT KELP of the Pacific is the longest seaweed. Its stalk may grow over 1,000 feet long. Narrow blades that grow along the stalk have round bladders at their base. The SEA COLLANDER, found in shallow or deep water off both coasts, has a blade that may be a foot wide and over 9 feet long. The blade has many holes and a strong rib running through the middle. It grows on a short, stout stalk. The WINGED KELP, found on both coasts, has a long blade with wavy or indented edges and a series of small narrow winglike blades at its base. It may grow 10 feet long on a stalk about a foot long.

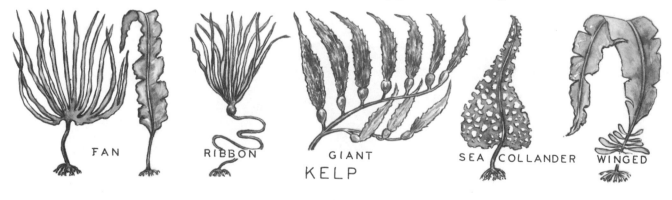

FAN   RIBBON   GIANT   SEA COLLANDER   WINGED

KELP

BLUE-GREEN AND GREEN ALGAE

BLUE-GREEN
ALGAE

MERMAID'S
HAIR

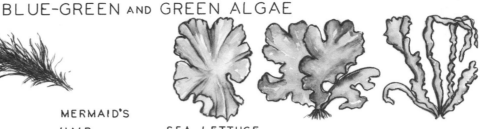

SEA LETTUCE

BLUE-GREEN ALGAE form a scum or fuzz on mud, rocks, or wood, often in polluted waters. The thread-like MERMAID'S HAIR is found in shallow water along both coasts. It is bluish-green; some of the other species in this blue-green group are red.

The other algae on this page are GREEN ALGAE.

SEA LETTUCE, which grows to 3 feet in length, is the largest green algae. Some kinds have broad ruffle-edged blades like lettuce; other kinds have narrow ribbon-like blades. The blades are either attached to some object in shallow water or floating. Some kinds are found on both coasts.

CODIUM   SEA MOSS

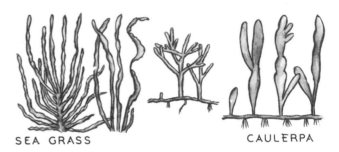

SEA GRASS   CAULERPA

CODIUM has greenish-black cylindrical branches with a spongy texture. It grows from 4 to 9 inches high along our southeastern, Gulf, and southwestern coasts. SEA MOSS has feathery dark green branches that grow from 2 to 8 inches long on rocks and wood along both coasts.

SEA GRASS has long narrow ribbon-like, or inflated, green blades. It grows along both coasts attached to stones or wood with the tips reaching the surface in shallow water. CAULERPA has 2 to 4 inch long green blades on a long stem growing on muddy or sandy bottoms on our southeastern coast.

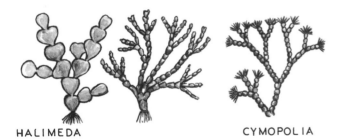

HALIMEDA   CYMOPOLIA

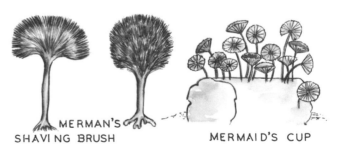

MERMAN'S
SHAVING BRUSH   MERMAID'S CUP

HALIMEDA is a low-growing cactus-like seaweed found along our southeastern and Gulf coasts. It has segmented branches that are hardened by limy deposits. CYMOPOLIA has rounded beadlike segmented branches that have a tuft of hair at the tips. It grows in shallow water on the south Florida coast.

MERMAN'S SHAVING BRUSH grows to 5 inches high in sand or mud. Its stalk is topped by a brushlike cluster of green filaments. MERMAID'S CUP grows 1 to 3 inches high on coral and debris. Its thin stalks have green umbrella- or cup-shaped tops. Both kinds are found in shallow water off Florida.

RED ALGAE

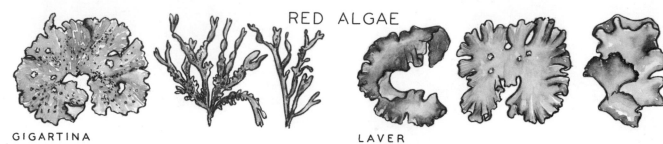

GIGARTINA

LAVER

GIGARTINA grows from 6 inches to 3 feet long in tide pools and on rocky shores along both coasts. Different kinds vary in shape from narrow, flat branches to a broad, rough blade. The color varies from bright red to black. Gigartina is used commercially as a source of gelatin.

LAVER in some forms looks like red sea lettuce; other forms have long blades with ruffled edges or twisted, ribbon-like blades. Laver grows with the holdfast attached to rock or wood along the northern Atlantic and the Pacific coasts. In many places it is eaten boiled or made into soup.

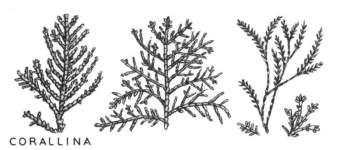

CORALLINA

POLYSIPHONIA

CORALLINA or CORAL ALGAE grows from 2 to 5 inches high on rocks in shallow and deeper water along both coasts. The fernlike branches are hard and brittle because they contain lime. The color varies from reddish-purple to grayish-green. Pieces washed up on beaches are usually bleached white.

POLYSIPHONIA or MANY-TUBED SEAWEED grows from 5 to 10 inches high on rocks and other seaweed in shallow or deep water. Several kinds are found along both coasts. This alga has finely divided branches that are hairlike in some species. The color varies from reddish-brown to black.

DASYA   **PLUMARIA**

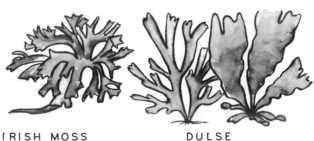

IRISH MOSS   **DULSE**

DASYA or CHENILLE WEED grows 2 or 3 feet or longer and is found on both coasts. Its red or pink stalk and branches are hairy or velvety. PLUMARIA or FEATHER WEED has feathery red branches. It grows in tufts in deep water off both coasts. Pieces are often washed up on beaches.

IRISH MOSS grows to 6 inches high on rocks or wood along both coasts. It has thick, purple or olive-green branches and is used for gelatin. DULSE has flat, leathery, red or purple blades with forked ends. It grows to 2 feet long and is found on both coasts. It is rich in iodine and is used as a food.

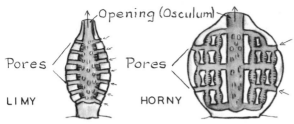

PARTS OF A SPONGE

GRANTIA   LEUCOSOLENIA

LIMY SPONGES

SPONGES

Sponges are a simple form of animal life. They are classified as Porifera, or pore-bearers, because their body wall has many small openings, or pores. There are hard, limy and glass sponges and soft horny sponges.

Water enters the sponge through the pores in the body wall. The water carries food and oxygen throughout the sponge and passes out through one or more openings at the top. The body wall contains minute needles (spicules) of lime or silica, or horny fibers to strengthen it and form the skeleton. The sponges that we find washed up on beaches or buy in stores consist of the skeleton only.

Sponges are found in both deep and shallow water and in warm and cold areas. They grow on some support such as rocks, wood, sand, shells, or seaweed. They may grow as single individuals or in masses. The largest sponges, including the commercial kinds, grow in deep, warm water.

A sponge reproduces by forming egg and sperm cells in its body. The cells unite and develop into tiny larvae which float out of the parent body into the water. The larvae swim about, then settle down and grow into sponges. Sometimes also a piece of old sponge breaks off and grows into a new one.

Two kinds of lime sponges are found off our northeastern coast. GRANTIA or URN SPONGES are gray, yellow, or reddish. They grow ½ to 1 inch high and are found around wharves and in tidal pools. LEUCOSOLENIA has whitish branches to 2 inches high. Other species of leucosolenia are found off the Pacific coast.

There are many kinds and shapes of horny sponges. The CRUMB-OF-BREAD SPONGE is gray or yellow and crumbly. It grows in small, low masses on stones or seaweed on both coasts.

The EYED FINGER SPONGE grows in bushy colonies along the northern Atlantic coast. It is orange-red when alive, white when washed ashore.

VASE or TUBE SPONGES are light brown and are found in warm eastern waters.

The REDBEARD SPONGE is bright orange-red. It grows in low masses on shells or wharves, or in clusters of fingers about 6 inches high along most of the Atlantic coast.

Among the commercial (bath) sponges found in deep, southern waters are the brown GLOVE SPONGE, the shaggy SHEEP'S WOOL SPONGE, and the soft GRASS SPONGE.

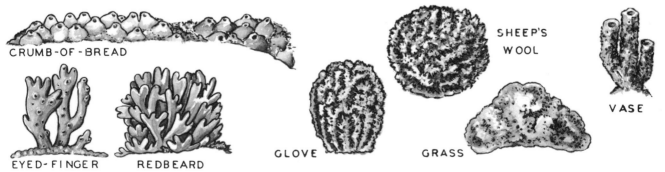

CRUMB-OF-BREAD

EYED-FINGER   REDBEARD

GLOVE   GRASS   SHEEP'S WOOL   VASE

HORNY SPONGES

Tentacles
Mouth
Circular muscle
Body wall
Long muscle
Basal disk

PARTS OF AN ANEMONE

Expanded　　Contracted

ANEMONE ON SHELL

SEA ANEMONES

Sea anemones are simple animals classified as Coelenterata, which means hollow gut or tube. The body of an anemone is a tube that has a mouth opening surrounded by tentacles at the top and a soft, slimy disk at the bottom. The flexible wall of the body tube has partitions that contain long muscles. When the muscles contract the tube is pulled down. A circular muscle near the top closes the mouth opening. When the anemone is disturbed or exposed by low tide, it pulls in its tentacles and contracts into a squashy mound. If touched it sends up bubbles and streams of water.

If the anemone wishes to move it can glide on its basal disk. When anchored in place, it is fastened firmly and hardly can be pried loose.

Anemones feed on small sea life such as microsopic animals, tiny crabs, shrimp, and small fishes. The tentacles around the anemone's mouth first paralyze the prey then draw it into the mouth opening. The tentacles can sting humans too.

Anemones sometimes multiply by forming buds that break off and become new individuals. They also produce eggs that develop into tiny, pear-shaped larvae. The larvae swim about for a week or so then settle down and grow into adults.

Anemones are found along both coasts in tidal pools, or on rocks, wood, or shells below the low water mark. The largest and most colorful varieties are found in warm water.

SAGARTIA are small anemones. One kind, found along the eastern coast, grows about 2 inches high and has a pinkish body with white tentacles. Another kind, found on both coasts, has a green body with orange stripes. It grows about ½ inch high.

ADAMSIA is a brownish anemone that attaches itself to the back of a shellfish or to the shell of a hermit crab. It grows to 3 inches in height and is found along the southern Atlantic coast.

ANTHOPLEURA is a green anemone that is found along the Pacific coast. It may grow to 12 inches high and 10 inches through. The green color is due to tiny algae that live in the body wall. The tentacles open in bright light and close at night, unlike most anemones which open in dim light.

METRIDIUM is the largest common anemone of the temperate regions of both coasts. When open it looks like a brown, pink, or white chrysanthemum with a thick, brown stem. It grows to be 4 inches high and 3 inches through.

METRIDIUM　　　　ANTHOPLEURA　　　　ADAMSIA　　　　SAGARTIA

SEA ANEMONES

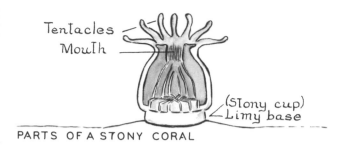

Tentacles
Mouth
(Stony cup)
Limy base

PARTS OF A STONY CORAL

STONY CORALS

Corals, like sea anemones, are coelenterates (hollow-tube animals). Stony corals have a soft body tube with a mouth opening and tentacles at the top. The base, or stony cup, is limy and is fastened to a support. Many individual animals grow close together in a colony to form one piece of coral. The corals that we find on beaches or in collections are the limy parts, or skeletons.

Coral animals feed on small, floating animal life which the tentacles collect. They usually are active at night. When they are exposed to bright light or disturbed the animals withdraw into the limy base.

Corals reproduce from eggs which develop into tiny larvae. The larvae glide about then settle on the bottom and grow into coral animals. Then each animal divides to form others and in this way large colonies are built up. In warm seas they form rock-like reefs and islands. In northern waters they form small patches on rocks or the sea bottom.

The white STAR CORAL grows ¼ inch high on stones and shells in shallow water along the East Coast.

The EYED CORAL grows in deep, cold water off the East Coast.

The BRAIN CORAL has a compact shape with many ridges. It grows to a large size in warm waters.

The STAGHORN CORAL, which grows in the form of white branches, is found off the Florida coast.

SEA PENS   SEA PANSIES   SEA FAN
HORNY CORALS

HORNY CORALS

These corals have a skeleton made of a horny substance instead of lime. They usually grow in the form of a stem with many branches. The animal parts, which are on the branches, have two forms, one with tentacles and one without. The form with tentacles takes in minute animal food, and the other form directs the flow of water.

The SEA FAN has a central stem and many fine branches that spread out like a fan. The branches are yellow, red, or purple, and the animal parts are white. It grows to 20 inches high in warm water off both of our coasts.

The SEA PEN has a stem with branches on either side like a fern. Different kinds are found along both of our coasts in deep water or in bays. They grow from 4 to 20 inches high and are orange, red, purple, green, or white in color.

The SEA PANSY is a squat form with a short stem and a broad top. The top is pinkish or violet, and the living animal parts, which cover it like a fringe, are white. Sea pansies are found on both coasts, where they live in the sand near the low-tide mark.

Living colony   Limy skeleton
STAR

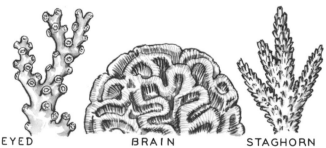

EYED   BRAIN   STAGHORN

STONY CORALS

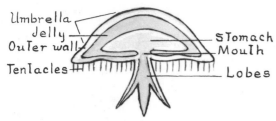

PARTS OF A JELLYFISH

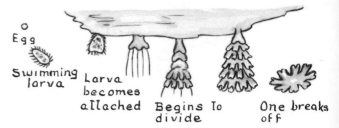

LIFE HISTORY OF THE MOON JELLY

JELLYFISHES

Jellyfishes, like anemones and corals, are hollow tube animals, coelenterates. The mouth of the jellyfish is on the underside and its tentacles hang down instead of standing up as in the anemone. The body part, which contains the jelly and acts as a float, is called the umbrella; the stomach and mouth are in the center and the tentacles hang below. Black dots around the edge act as eyes to tell light from dark.

Jellyfishes swim rather weakly by opening and closing the umbrella. They drift with the tides and are often washed ashore after a storm. They eat small sea creatures that they capture with their tentacles or mouth lobes and paralyze by stinging.

The way the white moon jelly reproduces is typical. In late summer or early fall eggs develop in the body of the female into tiny pear-shaped larvae with swimming hairs. The larvae swim away and settle on the bottom where they become attached at one end. Toward spring they grow longer and form layers. One layer after another breaks off, turns over and swims away. Each one grows into a full size jellyfish. By late summer each is ready to produce either sperm or egg cells and start a new life cycle. In the fall or winter it dies, a victim of storms.

The many different kinds of jellyfishes are shaped like bells, balls, cones, and disks. They vary in size from 1/16 of an inch to 8 feet across.

A transparent BELL JELLY seen under wharves on the Pacific coast is an inch or more across.

A ROUND JELLY found along the northern Atlantic coast is about ¾ of an inch across. Floating in the water it looks like a tiny, white balloon with a dark tail. The tail is a colony of individuals that feed and reproduce.

The WHITE or MOON JELLY is found along both the Atlantic and Pacific coasts. Its transparent umbrella grows to 10 or more inches across. It has a fringe of short tentacles around the edge and the dark outline of a four-leaf clover in the center. Four lobes with stinging cells hang below the mouth.

The GIANT PINK JELLY lives in the northern Atlantic, where it grows to 8 feet across in cold water, to 3 or 4 feet in temperate water. Its jelly part is thick and pinkish-brown at the center, thin and yellowish at the edges. Lobes and lappets hang from the mouth area. Stinging tentacles trail below the jelly part to a length of 75 or 100 feet.

BELL   ROUND   MOON or WHITE   GIANT PINK

JELLYFISHES

PORTUGUESE
MAN-OF-WAR

BY-THE-WIND-
SAILOR

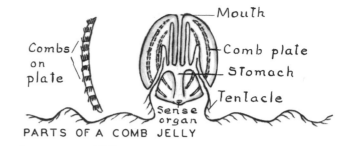

PARTS OF A COMB JELLY

JELLYFISH RELATIVES

The PORTUGUESE MAN-OF-WAR is a colony of individuals that hang beneath a gas-filled float. The float may be from 4 or 5 inches to 2 feet across. It is tinted in shades of rose and blue or green and has a reddish crest across the top. As it drifts with the wind it changes its shape. Tentacles to 50 feet long serve as a drag-anchor. The tentacles are poisonous to other sea creatures and to human swimmers. These jellyfish relatives are most numerous in warm seas, but some are found in the temperate Atlantic.

The BY-THE-WIND-SAILOR is another floating colony. It has a blue-green, gas-filled raft, 2 to 4 inches long, with a triangular sail set diagonally across it. Short tentacles that hang from the edge of the raft are moderately poisonous. By-the-wind-sailors live in warm waters along both coasts; some drift northward in the Gulf Stream.

COMB JELLIES

Comb jellies are not Coelenterata. They are Ctenophora, or comb-bearers. Along their jelly bodies they have rows of comb plates. Each plate moves up and down, one after the other, and propels the jelly through the water. As the plates move, they refract light and shine with changing colors—red, blue, and green. The tentacles, if any, of these jellies are not poisonous.

Comb jellies eat small shrimp, small fishes, and other tiny sea creatures that they catch with their sticky tentacles or in their wide mouths.

Each individual produces both egg and sperm cells. The fertilized eggs develop into tiny swimming larvae. After going through several changes the larvae grow into comb jellies.

The SEA GOOSEBERRY, just under an inch long, is transparent or yellowish and has two long tentacles. It is found off both coasts.

The SEA WALNUT is translucent and grows to 4 inches long. It is found off the middle part of the Atlantic and the California coasts.

The SEA EGG grows about 2 inches long and has two long pink tentacles. It is found along our northern Atlantic and Pacific coasts.

The SEA HELMET, pinkish and 1¼ inches long, has a wide mouth opening and no tentacles. It is found off the northeastern coast.

The VENUS GIRDLE is long and flat, like a ribbon. It curls and uncurls while moving through the water. The stomach and sense organs are in the middle and a double row of short tentacles around the edge. The tentacles reflect bands of colors. The kind of venus girdle found off the Atlantic coast grows to be 6 inches long.

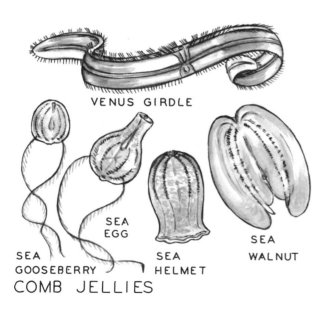

VENUS GIRDLE

SEA
EGG

SEA
GOOSEBERRY

SEA
HELMET

SEA
WALNUT

COMB JELLIES

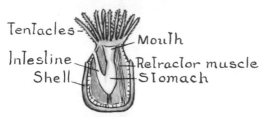

PARTS OF A MOSS ANIMAL

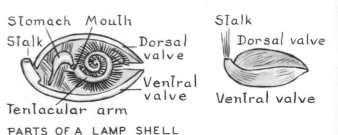

PARTS OF A LAMP SHELL

MOSS ANIMALS: BRYOZOA

These small sea animals belong to an ancient group. They live in colonies on rocks, wharfs, shells, seaweeds, or other objects in shallow or deep water along both coasts. They look more like seaweed than animals. Each individaul is so small that a magnifying lens is needed to see its structure. It has a horny or limy shell with an opening at one end. A ring of tentacles at the opening can be extended or withdrawn. When extended the tentacles collect plankton on which the animal feeds.

Moss animals increase when new individuals bud off the side of old ones. They also produce eggs that develop into swimming larvae. The larvae settle on an object and start a new colony.

There are several types of moss animals found along the Atlantic coast. The BRICK-RED kind which forms a rough crust on rocks or piles varies in color from white to orange to dark red. One kind of ALCYONIDIUM forms a jelly-like crust in shades of gray, yellow, red, and brown. Another kind has erect branches of a solid gelatinous material. TUFTED BUGULA has scaly, yellowish branches that grow to a height of 12 inches.

CRISIA, found along both coasts, is an upright, branched form a little under an inch high.

LAMP SHELLS: BRACHIOPODA

These shell animals belong to the same ancient group as the Bryozoa. Each animal has two shells and a stalk by which it is attached to a rock or other object. The shells are held together by a muscle at the stalk end. They open at the other end to let water enter. Inside the shells are a pair of tentacular arms coiled on two ridges. A fringe along the side of each arm waves to direct water with its tiny particles of food toward the mouth.

Lamp shells produce eggs which develop into swimming larvae; the larvae later attach to some object and develop into adults.

One kind of lamp shell, the LINGULA, has a stalk about 3 inches long and a shell about 1 inch long. It makes a narrow tunnel in wet sand and fastens its stalk at the lower end. It is found between tides in warm waters of the Pacific coast. Another kind of lamp shell, TEREBRATULINA, has an oval shell about ½ inch long. The under shell (ventral valve) is larger than the upper shell (dorsal valve), and it has a beak through which the stalk sticks out. The stalk fastens the shell to a rock. This lamp shell is found in shallow as well as deeper water along the Atlantic coast. Similar species are found in the Pacific Ocean.

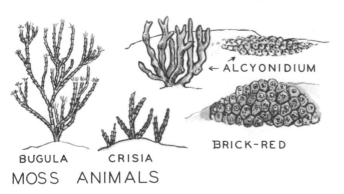

MOSS ANIMALS

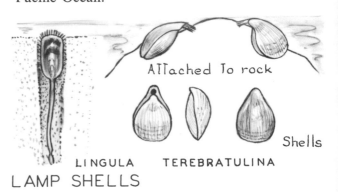

LAMP SHELLS

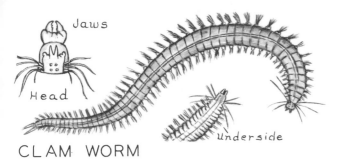

CLAM WORM

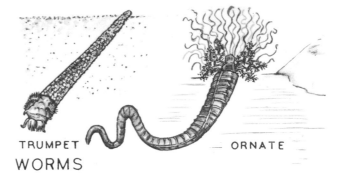

TRUMPET — ORNATE
WORMS

SEGMENTED SEA WORMS

Most segmented sea worms are classified as Polychaeta, meaning having many bristles. Each segment of the body may have a pair of fleshy lobes with bristles on them. The head end usually has tentacles and mouth parts. The worms are modified for swimming, burrowing, or living in tubes. They produce eggs which develop into top-shaped larvae. The larvae lengthen as they grow and become segmented.

SWIMMING AND BURROWING WORMS

The SAND WORM or CLAM WORM grows to 10 inches or longer. The male is bright blue-green. The female is dull green tinged with orange and red. During mating season on summer nights, these worms swim at the surface. Other times they live under rocks or in burrows in the sand in bays along our Pacific and northern Atlantic coasts. They feed on smaller worms and other sea creatures that they catch in their strong jaws. The jaws can be thrust out, then drawn with the food within the head.

The SEA MOUSE is from 3 to 6 inches long. The segments on its back are covered by brownish-gray, furlike hair. Along each side is a border of iridescent green and gold hairs and brown spines. This worm lives in sand and mud under shallow water along the Pacific and northern Atlantic coasts.

TUBE-BUILDING WORMS

These segmented worms build tubes to protect their bodies. The head end projects from the tube when the worm feeds and is drawn inside when it is disturbed.

The TRUMPET WORM makes a tube about 2 inches long from a single layer of sand. It digs in the sand by means of two sets of bristles in the shape of combs on each side of the head. Similar varieties of this worm are found along the Atlantic and Pacific coasts.

The TEREBELLID WORMS have thin tubes coated with mud, sand, or bits of shell. Different kinds of these worms are found along both of our coasts, chiefly in cooler water. One kind is the ORNATE WORM of the Atlantic coast, which grows to be 15 inches long. It has three pairs of feathery red gills and many thin yellowish tentacles on its head.

The FAN WORM, found in deep water along the northern Atlantic coast, grows from 12 to 15 inches long. It has a tough, papery tube. Two pale feathery fans with purple bands grow from its head.

The PLUMED WORM, found in crevices in rocks along the Pacific coast, has a tough, grayish tube that grows to be 18 inches long. When extended, the plumed gills on its head resemble a flower.

SEA MOUSE

FAN PLUMED
WORMS (Head end)

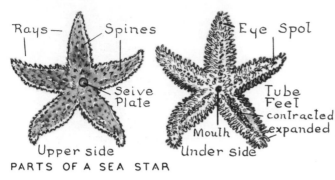

Rays — Spines   Eye Spot

Seive Plate

Tube Feet contracted expanded

Mouth

Upper side   Under side

PARTS OF A SEA STAR

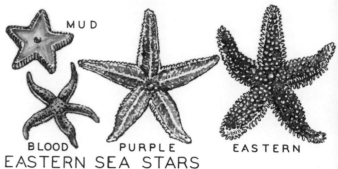

MUD

BLOOD   PURPLE   EASTERN

EASTERN SEA STARS

STARFISHES

Starfishes are echinoderms, or spiny-skinned animals. They have a flexible skeleton composed of small, limy plates connected by movable joints. Spines from the plates project through the skin of the upper side. The body has five or more rays.

On the underside of the rays are rows of tube feet which contract and expand enabling the starfish to move. At the end of each ray is a small eyespot that is sensitive to light. In the center of the underside is the mouth.

On the upper side near the center is a sieve plate (madreporite) through which water enters. The water passes through tubes in the body. Fingerlike projections in the skin are for breathing.

A starfish feeds chiefly on bivalve mollusks. It injects a fluid into them which relaxes the muscle that holds the shells together and pulls with its tube feet until the shells open. Then the starfish turns its stomach out through its mouth and inserts it between the shells.

Starfishes reproduce by means of eggs which are cast into the water or held under the body of the female. The eggs develop into swimming larvae which go through several changes then settle down and grow into starfishes. If a ray and part of the body of a starfish breaks off, it can grow into a new individual.

The MUD STAR is yellowish and 3 to 4 inches across. It is found all along the Atlantic coast in both shallow and deep water.

The BLOOD STAR may be red, purple, orange, or cream. It grows from 2½ to 4 inches across and is found along rocky coasts of the northern Atlantic.

The PURPLE STAR, which grows from 6 to 12 inches across, is common off the northeastern coast.

The COMMON or EASTERN STAR is reddish-brown, purple, green, or orange. It is 6 to 11 inches across and may have more or less than five rays. It is common along the Atlantic coast, where it is very destructive to oyster beds.

The SEA BAT is red, yellow, or purple. It has blunt rays and grows to 7 inches across. It is found in tide pools and deep water along the Pacific coast.

The RED STAR has slender pointed rays and grows to 4 inches across. It is found along the Pacific coast, except the southernmost part.

The OCHRE STAR is brown, yellow, or purple and from 6 to 14 inches across. It is the common star of the Pacific coast.

Egg   Developing Larva

LIFE HISTORY OF A SEA STAR

SEA BAT

RED   OCHRE

WESTERN SEA STARS

PURPLE   COMMON   SUNFLOWER

SUN STARS

SUN STARS

These are large starfishes which have many rays. Some species develop directly from egg to starfish without any swimming larva stage.

The PURPLE SUN STAR has from seven to thirteen rays and grows from 16 to 20 inches across. Its spiny upper side is reddish-purple with yellow on the edges. It is found in shallow water along the northern Atlantic coast.

The COMMON SUN STAR looks like a colorful, crocheted doily. It has from eight to fourteen rays and is about 14 inches across. It comes in shades of red or pink or purple. It is found in both shallow and deep water of the northern Atlantic and Pacific.

The SUNFLOWER STAR starts with six rays. With age, it may have as many as twenty-four rays and grow to a width of 2 feet or more. It is found off rocky shores all along the Pacific coast.

BRITTLE STARS

This kind of starfish has a small body disc and five long jointed arms. The tube feet on each side of the arms are breathing and sense organs. The starfish pulls itself around by means of its flexible arms. The arms also capture food (plankton, small shellfish, and plant and animal matter).

Brittle star eggs hatch into swimming larvae which later change into small stars. It usually takes them two or three years to reach full size.

The GREEN BRITTLE STAR is ½ inch across the body and about 3 inches long on each arm. The northern Atlantic species usually is green or olive-brown with brown bands on the arms. The southern species is bright green with white bands.

The LONG ARMED SNAKE STAR has a very small body and threadlike arms 1½ inches long. It is grayish and is found along the northeastern coast.

The LITTLE SPINY STAR is about ½ inch across the body and 2½ inches along each arm. The body and arms have bristly spines. The arms have bands of different colors. Individuals of almost any hue can be found along the southeastern coast. A similar species is found on the Pacific coast.

The DAISY BRITTLE STAR is nearly an inch across the body and 3½ inches long in the arms. The colors vary, but all have different color bands on the arms. This star is found in both shallow and deep water off the northern Atlantic and Pacific coasts.

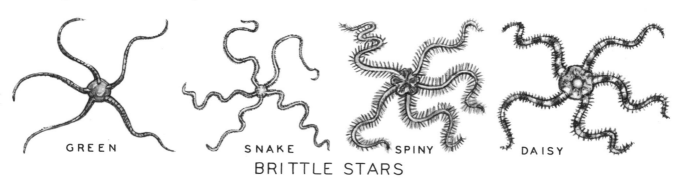

GREEN   SNAKE   SPINY   DAISY

BRITTLE STARS

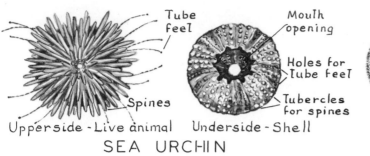

SEA URCHIN

Upperside - Live animal   Underside - Shell

Tube feel · Spines · Mouth opening · Holes for Tube feet · Tubercles for spines

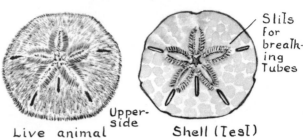

KEYHOLE URCHIN

Live animal   Upperside   Shell (Test)

Slits for breathing Tubes

SEA URCHINS

The sea urchin is a spiny-skinned animal (echinoderm). Its skeleton is a shell (test) made of small, limy plates joined together. Movable spines cover most of the shell. Five bands of tube feet pass around the shell between the spines. The urchin moves on the tube feet which are long and slender and have suction discs on the ends. With its sharp spines and its teeth the urchin makes a hollow in a rock into which it can wedge its shell.

In the center of the shell on the underside is the mouth which has five strong teeth. The teeth are used to crush the small mollusks, cut up the seaweeds, and scrape up the algae that the urchin eats.

To reproduce, urchins shed eggs and sperm into the water. The eggs develop into larvae which drift for a while, then settle on the bottom and grow into the adult form.

Different kinds of urchins are found along all of our coasts. They vary in size from 1½ to 10 inches across. Their spines may be long or short, thick or thin. In color they may be red, green, brown, purple, or yellow. Some kinds have poisonous spines. Urchins should not be picked up by hand or stepped on with bare feet. They can be found in warm or cool, deep or shallow water.

KEYHOLE URCHIN AND SAND DOLLAR

The KEYHOLE URCHIN has a flattened shell, or test, with five holes near the edge. The shell is covered by fine short spines. The urchin also has many short tube feet, and it moves slowly on the feet and spines. Most of the time it lies partly buried in the sand. It is found off the southeastern coast.

The SAND DOLLAR, which is found in shallow water along the northern Atlantic and Pacific coasts, is similar but does not have holes in its shell. The sand dollar and keyhole urchin both grow about 3 inches across the shell.

SEA CUCUMBERS

Sea cucumbers are another kind of Echinoderm. They resemble stout worms and have leathery skin with a few limy plates scattered through it. They are able to expand and contract, and they move by means of the rows of tube feet on their underside. The tube feet on the upper side are used for feeling and breathing. Tentacles around the mouth gather in the food—bits of living or dead organisms.

Sea cucumbers live in sand or under rocks in cool water along both coasts. Different kinds grow from 2 to 18 inches long and are red, brown, blue, or green in color.

Tentacles · Mouth · Tube feet

THYONE   WESTERN CUCUMERIA

Contracted · Expanded · NORTHERN CUCUMERIA

SEA CUCUMBERS

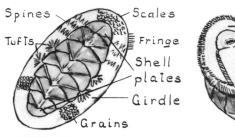

PARTS OF A CHITON

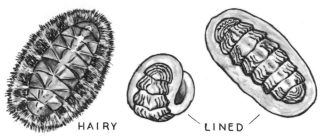

CHITONS or SEA CRADLES

MOLLUSKS

A mollusk has a soft body that is usually protected by a hard shell. The shell is made from the lime in the water by a part of the body called the mantle. The mantle keeps adding to the shell making it larger until the mollusk is full grown.

CHITONS

The most primitive living mollusk is the CHITON or SEA CRADLE. Its oval body is covered by a shell made of eight overlapping plates that are held together by a tough, leathery girdle. Separate plates are often washed up on the beach. Some shaped like wings are called butterfly shells; others resemble a set of false teeth.

The chiton glides on the bottom, or foot, of its body when it moves about to feed on algae at night. During the day it usually stays in one spot, firmly clamped to a rock or other support.

Female chitons lay eggs which hatch into swimming larvae that soon change into young chitons. In some kinds the young live under the mantle edge of the female.

Chitons usually live in colonies in crevices in rocks in shallow water. They are found along both coasts. Different kinds grow from ¾ of an inch to 12 or more inches long. They are brown, gray, or black with markings of blue, green, orange, or red. Some kinds have a spiny border (girdle), others have a smooth or a grainy border.

8 PLATES OF CHITON SHELL

TUSK OR TOOTH SHELLS

These mollusks are in a class by themselves; they are Scaphopoda, or spade-footed animals. They have a slender, soft body inside a long tusk-shaped shell that has an opening at each end. The head and foot parts are at the larger end. The muscular, cylindrical foot extends from the shell and digs into the bottom sand or mud pulling the shell downward until only the small opening is exposed to the water. Thread-like tentacles around the mouth feel around in the sand and capture the minute organisms that are used as food.

The females lay eggs which develop into tiny creatures having cup-shaped shells in two parts. As the shells grow the parts unite and form a long tube or tusk.

Tusk shells are found along both of our coasts, some kinds in shallow water, some in deep water. The shells are light colored and from ½ to 5 inches long. The Indians of the Northwest made them into beads and used them for money (wampum).

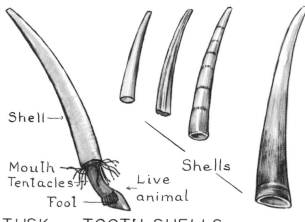

TUSK or TOOTH SHELLS

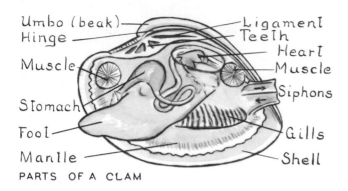

PARTS OF A CLAM

HARD-SHELL CLAM or QUAHOG

BIVALVE OR PELECYPOD MOLLUSKS

The body of a bivalve or pelecypod (hatchet-footed) mollusk is covered by two shells, or valves, which are joined at the top, or small end, by a hinge and ligament. A strong muscle in each side of the shells controls their closing.

When the shells are open the hatchet-shaped foot sticks out of one side. The foot is used to pull the bivalve around when it wants to move. Opposite the foot two siphons, or necks, protrude. One siphon takes in water and the other passes it out. The water provides oxygen for breathing and small particles of plant and animal life for food.

The shell is made by the mantle, a fold of skin that covers the body. It secretes a horny substance and adds lime from the water to it. The more lime it uses the heavier the shell becomes.

Bivalve mollusks lay eggs that are either set free in the water or held in the gills of the female until they hatch into minute larvae. The larvae have waving hairs with which they swim. After they grow and develop two shells, they settle down and take on the adult form.

EDIBLE CLAMS

The HARD-SHELL CLAM or QUAHOG is found on sandy or muddy bottoms along the Atlantic coast. It has a heavy, grayish-white shell that grows to be 5 or 6 inches across. Half-grown clams are sold as cherrystones, or little-necks.

The SOFT-SHELL or LONG-NECK CLAM buries itself in mud or sand above the low tide mark. Its white shell grows to a length of 4 inches. Its long neck, or siphon, sticks up into the water. It is native to the East and is cultivated on the West Coast.

The PISMO CLAM is found in sand on exposed beaches from mid-California southward. Its shiny shell is light brown with purple markings. This clam grows to a length of 7 inches.

The GEODUCK of the Pacific coast is the largest of our clams. Its shell is 8 inches or longer and it weighs up to 12 pounds. It lives in a burrow in sand or mud, and its long neck reaches to the surface.

A RAZOR CLAM has an elongated shell and a strong foot with which it can dig rapidly under the sand. The common Atlantic variety has a greenish-brown shell 6 or 7 inches long.

CLAMS

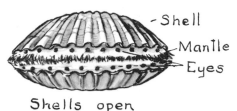

Shells open

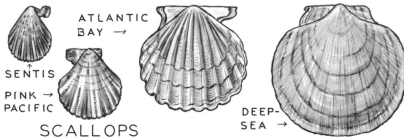

SENTIS

PINK → PACIFIC

ATLANTIC BAY →

DEEP-SEA →

SCALLOPS

SCALLOPS

Scallops take their name from the wavy edge of their shell. The shell has a wing, or ear, on one or both sides of the hinge. Different kinds vary in size from 1 to 8 inches across. In color they are shades of red, purple, yellow, brown, or white, sometimes with darker bands. The lower shell, on which the scallop lies on the sea bottom, is flatter than the upper shell and usually covered with green scum.

When the shells are open the two borders of the mantle show. The edges are fringed and there is a row of blue eyes along each border. The eyes can see well enough to warn the shells when to close, and to guide in swimming. The scallop swims a zig-zag course by opening and closing its shells, taking in and shooting out water. Sometimes a whole school swims to the surface at one time.

The large muscle that controls the closing of the shells is the part that we eat. Edible scallops are found off both of our coasts. The ATLANTIC BAY SCALLOP is 2 or 3 inches; the DEEP SEA SCALLOP is 5 to 8 inches. The GIANT PACIFIC SEA SCALLOP is about 7 inches across.

Among the many small, brightly-colored scallops are the Atlantic SENTIS SCALLOP, which has one right ear and is 1 inch across, and the PACIFIC PINK SCALLOP 2 inches across, with one left ear.

OYSTERS

The COMMON OYSTER is one of our most valuable shellfishes. It is native to the Atlantic coast and is cultivated along the Pacific coast. Its light gray, rough, heavy shell grows from 6 to 10 inches long. The convex lower shell is cemented to some solid object; the upper shell is flatter and smaller.

The female oyster produces millions of eggs that hatch in a few hours into swimming larvae. The larvae soon form shells, settle on old shells or some other hard surface and begin to grow. In two years they are mature; but, since they have many enemies, many never reach this state.

The native PACIFIC OYSTER is also eaten although it is much smaller.

SPINY (THORNY) OYSTERS or CHRYSANTHEMUM SHELLS are colorful and popular with shell collectors. They live in fairly deep water where they are attached to rocks or wrecks. The Atlantic species grows 3 or 4 inches long, the Pacific kind to 5 inches.

JEWEL BOXES are other kinds of oyster shells that are often collected. Outside they have ruffles and spines and are yellow, orange, red, or white. Inside they are pearly pink, purple, or yellow. They grow 1 or 2 inches long in rather deep water off the southern Atlantic coast.

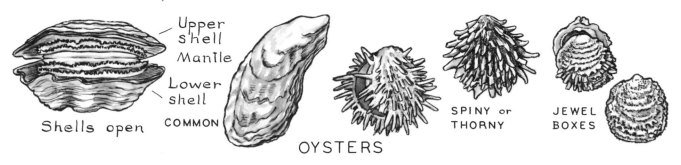

Upper shell

Mantle

Lower shell

Shells open

COMMON

SPINY or THORNY

JEWEL BOXES

OYSTERS

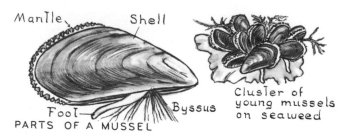

PARTS OF A MUSSEL

Cluster of young mussels on seaweed

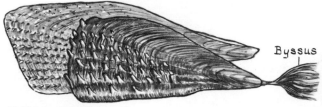

PEN SHELLS

MUSSELS

Mussels live in masses on piers, rocks, and mud flats along all of our coasts. Although they can move about on their slender foot, they usually stay in one place. Glands in the foot spin a set of strong byssus threads by which the shells are attached to some support. The mussel has a pair of wedge-shaped shells that are dark colored on the outside and pearly inside.

The BLUE MUSSEL lives along the northern and central parts of our Atlantic and Pacific coasts. It grows 2 or 3 inches long and is bluish-black on the outside, white with a violet border inside. This is the mussel that is most often eaten.

The RIBBED MUSSEL is yellowish or greenish. It lives on mud flats along the temperate Atlantic coast and grows to 3 inches long. It is not edible.

The CALIFORNIA MUSSEL forms large beds in surf-swept areas along the Pacific coast from Alaska to Mexico. Its shell has ribs along the middle and coarse growth lines. It grows from 2 to 10 inches in length.

The DATE MUSSEL, so called because of its shape and color, lives on a rock in a hollow that it makes by means of an acid secretion. It grows to be 2 inches long off the southern Pacific coast and to 5 inches in the Gulf of Mexico.

The BENT or HOOKED MUSSEL has a ridged, dark purple or brown shell 1 or 2 inches long. It is found in the temperate and warm water of the Atlantic.

The HORSE MUSSEL has a large, heavy, brownish to bluish-black shell. The Atlantic kind grows to be 5 or 6 inches long and the Pacific kind to 9 inches. These mussels live in deep water where they anchor themselves to the bottom by making a nest of pebbles and bits of shell held together with byssus threads.

PEN SHELLS

The pen shell is another wedge-shaped shell. Its small end is tapered and has a tassel of byssus threads attached to it. The threads are made by the foot part of the body; they are fine, silky, and golden in color.

The two kinds of pen shells commonly found off the southern Atlantic coast live in deep water on sandly or muddy bottoms; the pointed end is buried and is fastened to a stone or shell by byssus threads. Empty shells are often washed up on beaches. They are from 5 to 9 inches long and are light or dark brown. Ridges, more spiny in one kind than the other, run the length of the shell. The large muscle that holds the two shells together is eaten like that of the scallop.

BLUE   RIBBED

DATE

CALIFORNIA

HOOKED

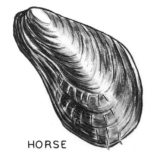

HORSE

MUSSELS

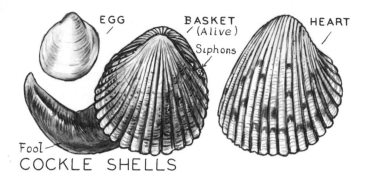

COCKLE SHELLS

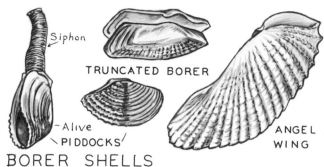

BORER SHELLS

COCKLE AND JINGLE SHELLS

Cockle shells are rounded and usually have scalloped edges. The BASKET COCKLE, common off the Pacific coast, has a ribbed grayish or brownish shell from 3 to 6 inches long. It has a very large foot with which it digs into the sandy bottom. The GREAT HEART COCKLE, 4 or 5 inches long, is the large common cockle of the Atlantic coast. The shell is yellowish-brown with streaks of dark purple-brown on the outside and pink inside. The EGG COCKLES of the Atlantic coast have smooth, shiny shells 1 or 2 inches long. They are white, yellow, or pinkish.

Jingle shells have a convex upper shell and a smaller and flatter lower shell. The lower shell has a hole for the byssus threads which attach it to a rock, other shells, seaweeds, or pilings. The upper shell is often washed ashore. The PLAIN JINGLE SHELL, found in rather deep water off the Atlantic coast, is pearly yellow or gray and 1 inch or more across. The PERUVIAN JINGLE SHELL of the south California coast is similar. The FALSE JINGLE SHELL found along the Pacific coast grows to be 4 inches long and is rough on the outside, pearly inside. A similar species is found off Florida.

BORER AND ARK SHELLS

Borers have a pair of matching shells with a long and a short end. The short end has sharp ridges or teeth which it uses to bore into sand, mud, or rock.

The PIDDOCK has a round foot that acts as a suction cup to fasten it to the rock while the shell bores. The Atlantic species grows to 2 inches and the Pacific species grows to 4½ inches in length.

The TRUNCATED BORER is 2 to 3 inches long and the ANGEL WING, 4 to 8 inches. Both have beautiful white ridged shells and are found along the Atlantic coast. Similar, but less handsome, species live in the Pacific.

Ark shells are heavy and long or rounded. All have a long hinge with an even row of teeth. The CUT-RIBBED ARK of the southeastern coast is white and from 2½ to 5 inches in length. The BLOOD ARK is 2 or 3 inches long and is common off the temperate Atlantic coast. Its rounded shell has flat ribs and a brown, shaggy skin on the lower part. The animal is one of the few mollusks to have red blood. The TURKEY WING shell, found in the warmer waters of the Atlantic coast, is 2 or 3 inches long. It is yellow or grayish with brown stripes. It lives attached to rocks by a silken byssus cord.

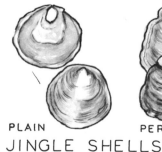

PLAIN   PERUVIAN   FALSE

JINGLE SHELLS

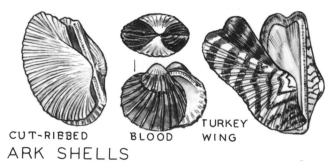

CUT-RIBBED   BLOOD   TURKEY WING

ARK SHELLS

PANDORA SHELLS   THRACIA

PANDORA SHELLS have thin flattened white valves (shells) from 1 to 2 inches long. The right valve is flatter than the left. THRACIA SHELLS are white or grayish and from 1 to 4 inches long. The beak of the right valve has a hole. Some kinds of both shells are found along both of our coasts.

TELLIN SHELLS

TELLIN SHELLS are translucent, shiny, and from ¼ to 4 inches long. Some are white or yellow; some have bands or rays of rose or purple. A few kinds of these beautiful little shells are found along our warmer Pacific coast; more kinds are found along the southern Atlantic coast.

VENUS CLAMS

These VENUS CLAM shells are mostly white; some have blotches of color. The first two, about 2 inches long, are the FRILLED and the COMMON CALIFORNIA VENUS. The second two are the IMPERIAL and the CROSSBARRED VENUS, which are about an inch long and are found along the southeastern coast.

CHESTNUT CLAMS

CHESTNUT CLAMS are ½ to 2 inches long. Their heavy shells are brown on the outside, white inside. Some are nearly smooth, some deeply ridged. The animals inside are orange or red. Some kinds of these clams are found in deep, some in shallow, water along the Atlantic coast and off Alaska.

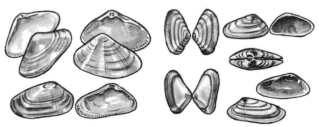

WEDGE and BUTTERFLY (COQUINA) SHELLS

WEDGE SHELLS, ¾ to 1 inch long, are white or brownish, some with darker rays. They are found in shallow water along both coasts. BUTTERFLY or COQUINA SHELLS, ½ to ¾ of an inch long, come in many colors and patterns, seldom two alike. They are found on sandy shores of the southern Atlantic.

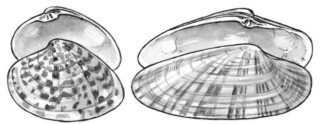

CALICO CLAM   SUNRAY SHELL

The CALICO CLAM has a glossy shell that is cream colored with brown markings, from 1½ to 2½ inches long. SUNRAY SHELLS are glossy and 4 or 5 inches long. They are pinkish, gray, and lavender with darker rays. Both kinds of shells are fairly common along some parts of the southeastern coast.

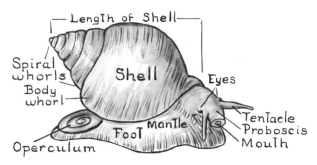

PARTS OF A UNIVALVE MOLLUSK or SEA SNAIL

PERIWINKLES

UNIVALVE OR GASTROPOD MOLLUSKS

Univalve or gastropod (stomach-in-the-foot) mollusks are sea snails of many different shapes and sizes. The snail's body is usually covered by one valve, or shell, which most often has a coiled form. The lower part of the body is a large, muscular foot on which the snail glides. On the back of the foot is a horny operculum that closes the shell opening when the snail draws its body inside. The head has two feelers, or tentacles, with the eyes at the base of the tentacles or on stalks. The mouth is at the base of the tentacles or on a snout (or proboscis). Inside the mouth is a coiled tongue (radula) edged with many sharp teeth. The tongue rolls over the food and scrapes it up or shreds it. Some snails eat plants, others eat animal food.

The snail's body is encased by a mantle which lines the shell and is attached to it in one place. The mantle makes the shell by using lime from sea water. A smooth-edged mantle makes a smooth shell, an irregular edge makes an irregular shell. In some snails, part of the mantle is rolled to form a siphon tube. Sea snails reproduce by laying eggs which either develop directly into tiny snails or first go through two larval stages.

PERIWINKLES AND MOON SHELLS

Periwinkles are common little grayish or brown snails that live on rocks above or below the high tide mark along both coasts. They feed on algae. By closing the operculum they can live out of water for some time. COMMON and ANGULATE PERIWINKLES grow about an inch long and live on the Atlantic coast. The CHECKERED PERIWINKLE of the Pacific has white spots on its brown or black shell and grows about ½ inch long.

The LARGE MOON SHELLS found along the Atlantic and Pacific coasts are light grayish-brown and 3 or 4 inches high. The moon shell snail has a very large foot with which it burrows into moist sand making a mound that shows at low tide. It also uses its foot to grasp other shells while it drills a hole in them with its tongue in order to feed on the animal inside.

The moon snail lays its eggs in a gluey substance that it molds around its shell then casts off. Sand sticks to the gluey material and stiffens it into the shape of a collar.

The following three moon shells are found on the Atlantic coast. The SHARK'S EYE is 1 or 2 inches high and is bluish-brown with a dark brown spot. The COLORFUL MOON is the same size and is light bluish with brown or purple markings. The SPOTTED MOON is ½ inch high and gray with brown spots.

SAND COLLARS

LARGE MOON SNAIL

MOON SHELLS

SHARK'S EYE   SPOTTED

COLORFUL

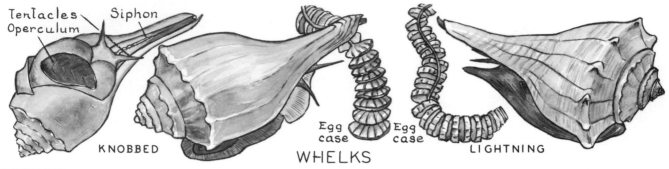

Tentacles
Operculum
Siphon

Egg case   Egg case

KNOBBED   WHELKS   LIGHTNING

WHELKS

Whelks have large, more-or-less pear-shaped shells. Most kinds have a long canal at one end with a siphon under it. As the whelk slides through sand and mud the siphon is turned up to take in clear water.

The whelk preys on other mollusks. To get into snail shells it drills a hole with its tongue. With clams, it inserts its own shell between the other's two.

The KNOBBED WHELK's shell is from 5 to 9 inches long. It is grayish on the outside and yellow or red inside. Young shells have violet streaks on the outside. The body whorl is crowned by a row of blunt knobs. The opening, on the right side, may be closed by a horny, pear-shaped operculum.

The CHANNELED WHELK grows 5 to 7 inches long. Its shell is grayish on the outside, yellow inside; the spire has five or six flattened whorls with a deep groove at the base of each.

The LIGHTNING or LEFT-HANDED WHELK grows from 4 to 16 inches long. Its shell is yellow and brown inside. On the outside it is grayish with wavy, purple-brown markings like streaks of lightning. Each streak passes through a blunt knob at the crown of the large body whorl. The opening is on the left side.

The females of the knobbed, channeled, and lightning whelks lay their eggs in a long string of horny cases. The string is attached to some object under the water and may be from 9 inches to 2 feet or longer. Each case contains several eggs. After a few weeks the eggs hatch into tiny whelks which make a hole in each case and crawl out.

Knobbed and channeled whelks are found along most of our Atlantic shore. They are edible and are sometimes sold in southern markets. The lightning whelk is found in the warmer waters of the Atlantic.

The PEAR WHELK, which lives in clear shallow water in the southern Atlantic, has a shell with a rather short, blunt spire. It grows 3 or 4 inches long and is light gray with brown markings.

The WAVED WHELK shell is from 2 to 4 inches long and is brown on the outside with many ridges. It comes from shallow or deep water in the northern Atlantic.

The TEN-RIDGED WHELK lives in deep water off the northeastern coast. Its shell grows to 4 inches long and is light gray with brown spiral ridges.

The TABLED WHELK lives in deep water off the Pacific coast. Its shell is 4 or 5 inches long and is light yellow; the spire has flat channels with scalloped edges.

CHANNELED   PEAR   WAVED   TEN-RIDGED   TABLED

WHELKS (Shells)

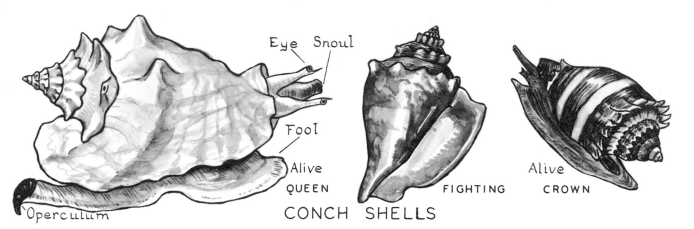

Eye Snoul

Fool

Alive
QUEEN

Operculum

Alive
FIGHTING

Alive
CROWN

CONCH SHELLS

CONCH SHELLS

Conch are large snails with heavy shells. They are found in shallow water in the warmer parts of the Atlantic.

The QUEEN or GIANT CONCH SHELL, found off the Florida coast, grows to be a foot long. It is yellowish on the outside; inside the flaring lip, it is pink, yellow, and orange. The body whorl has a row of large knobs around the shoulder. The animal in the shell has a large, muscular foot on which it glides or leaps. It is a scavenger and eats dead animal food.

The FIGHTING CONCH SHELL grows 3 or 4 inches long. It has a large outer lip and a row of spines on the shoulder of the body whorl. Its color varies from orange to purple-brown with light and dark markings. This conch feeds on other shell animals which it attacks by leaping from side to side.

The CROWN CONCH is another fighter. It even attacks shell animals that are larger than itself. Its shell grows from 2 to 5 inches long. It has a row of spines at the shoulder, and usually another at the base, of the body whorl. In color it has a varied pattern with bands of bluish, white, purple, and shades of brown.

The HORSE CONCH, which grows to be 2 feet long, is the largest snail in our waters. The shell has a long spire and a long canal. It is sculptured with wavy ridges and raised ribs and is covered by a reddish-brown skin. Young shells are bright orange-red. The snail's body is bright red and when extended is much larger than the shell. When it feeds on other conch and large shell animals, it wraps its large foot around them. The female lays eggs in rows of cone-shaped capsules.

The TULIP SHELLS are related to the horse conch, but they are much smaller and are not fighters. They feed mostly on dead animal matter. The TRUE TULIP is light gray with a varied pattern of orange, brown, or purple markings, and closely-spaced spiral lines. It grows to 5 inches long. The BANDED TULIP grows about 3 inches long. It has a smooth shell with streaks of brown and white and brown spiral lines.

Egg capsules

Alive

Alive
BANDED

TRUE

HORSE CONCH

TULIP SHELLS

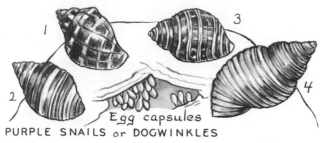

PURPLE SNAILS or DOGWINKLES

BASKET SHELLS   OYSTER DRILLS

PURPLE SNAILS or DOGWINKLES are small whelks that live on rocks, where they lay their eggs in capsules. The shells vary in shape and color even in one species. 1) and 2) are Atlantic coast species that grow 1 or 2 inches long. 3) and 4) live on the Pacific coast. 3) is 1 inch long and 4) 3 inches.

BASKET SHELLS are small whelks that live along muddy or sandy shores, 1) and 2) on the Atlantic coast, 3) on the Pacific coast. OYSTER DRILLS grow about an inch long. They live on the Atlantic and have been introduced on the Pacific coast. They bore into bivalve shells and eat the insides.

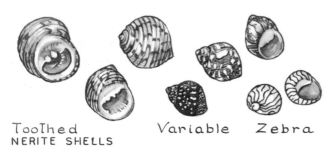

Toothed
NERITE SHELLS   Variable   Zebra

BUBBLE SHELLS

NERITE SHELLS. The TOOTHED variety has a ridged white shell with black and red markings. The VARIABLE kind has a smooth white shell with finely lined black markings. The ZEBRA is smooth and white with black lines. All are small and are found along our southern Atlantic shore.

BUBBLE SHELLS are thin and oval with a long opening. They have a short spire or none. Some kinds are found along all of our coasts, most of them in warm, shallow water. The shells are from less than ½ inch to 2 inches long. The snails' bodies are larger than the shells.

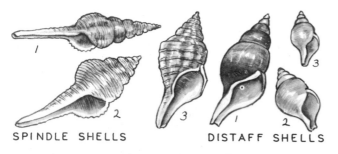

SPINDLE SHELLS   DISTAFF SHELLS

TURRET,   HORN,   STAIRCASE SHELLS

SPINDLE SHELLS have a long spire and a long canal. They grow 3 or 4 inches long. 1) and 2) are found in the Gulf of Mexico. 3) is found in the Pacific. DISTAFF SHELLS are more stocky. 1) grows to 3 inches, 2) to 2 inches, 3) to 1 inch long. They are found in deep water in the cooler Atlantic.

TURRET SHELLS have long, pointed spires and small openings. HORN SHELLS have knobbed or beaded spiral rows. STAIRCASE or WENTLETRAP SHELLS have rows of ridges on each whorl. All three kinds grow from about ½ to 2 inches long; some are found on the warmer parts of each coast.

LIMPETS

Atlantic   Pacific

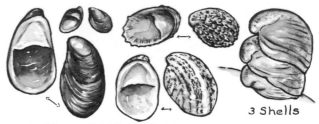

SLIPPER or BOAT SHELLS   3 Shells

LIMPETS have low, cone-shaped shells, some kinds with a hole in the top. They are found along both coasts. They grow from less than ½ to 4 inches long, the PACIFIC GIANT KEYHOLE being the largest. Most limpets live on rocks. They move to find plant food, but finally return to their original spots.

SLIPPER OR BOAT SHELLS are light gray or brown, convex or flattened, with a deck, or shelf, inside. Different kinds grow from ¼ to 2 inches long. They are found along both coasts attached to rocks, other shells, or seaweed. These snails feed on small particles taken from water passing through the gills.

←Alive

ABALONES

TOP SHELLS   **STAR** and **TURBAN SHELLS**

ABALONES are large limpet-like snails that live on rocks along the Pacific coast. Different kinds grow from 4 to 12 inches long. They are rough on the outside, pearly and bright colored on the inside. A row of holes along one side is used for breathing. These snails feed on algae.

TOP SHELLS are shaped like a pyramid and are from ½ to 4 inches long. TURBAN SHELLS are usually rough on the outside, pearly inside, and 1 or 2 inches long. Some kinds of top and turban shells are found along both coasts. White STAR SHELLS, 1 or 2 inches long, are found off Florida.

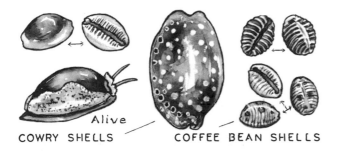

Alive

COWRY SHELLS   **COFFEE BEAN SHELLS**

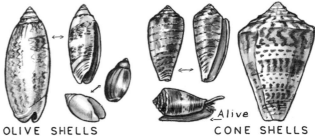

Alive

OLIVE SHELLS   **CONE SHELLS**

COWRY and COFFEE BEAN SHELLS are found in warm water on both coasts. They have one body whorl and no spire (except in young shells). Cowry shells are smooth and the snail has a large mantle that spreads over the shell. They grow from 1 to 5 inches long. Coffee bean shells are ½ inch long.

OLIVE SHELLS are smooth, oval, and ½ to 2½ inches long. The snail's body when extended is larger than the shell. CONE SHELLS are 1 to 3 inches long and are yellow or brown with varied markings. Olive and cone shells are found on both coasts; the large, colorful ones live in the southern Atlantic.

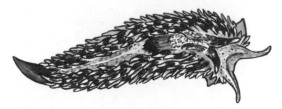

PLUMED SEA SLUG

NOBLE DORIS

SEA SLUGS: NUDIBRANCHS

Nudibranchs are sea snails which do not have an external shell. (In the embryo stage they have a small coiled shell.) Instead of internal gills they have projections on the back that serve as breathing organs. They creep over rocks, seaweed, or the bottom of the sea where they feed on small animal life and algae. They lay eggs in coiled strings on rocks, seaweed or other supports. A number of different kinds of nudibranchs, many of them brilliantly colored, are found along both of our coasts, usually in cold water.

The PLUMED SEA SLUG has rows of small, finger-like projections along its back which it uses for breathing, and two pairs of tentacles on its head. It grows to 4 inches in length and is orange or gray spotted with white, or green and purple. It is found in tide pools and deeper water along the Atlantic coast from Rhode Island northward.

The BUSHY-BACKED SEA SLUG is found on rocks and seaweed in the same area. Along the back it has two rows of transparent, treelike projections, which are its breathing organs. The head has branched appendages instead of tentacles. This slug is pale red or brownish with yellow or white spots and is about 2 inches long.

The DORID SEA SLUGS have breathing organs in a leaflike cluster at the rear end of the back. Several kinds of dorids are found along both of our coasts. Some kinds, which have a fruity odor and a yellow color, are called SEA LEMONS. The NOBLE DORIS, which is often found in tide pools along the Pacific coast, grows to 4 inches in length. It is yellowish with brown markings and reddish spots. It has a cluster of six ruffled, leaflike breathing organs on the back and two tentacles on the head.

SEA HARE

This slug has a rabbit-like appearance with its two large tentacles that look like ears, its oval-shaped body, and its yellowish or brown color. Some kinds of sea hares can swim as well as creep. Two rows of ruffled lobes along the back act as fins. A siphon between the lobes squirts out a cloud of purple ink when the slug is disturbed. A small, flat, horny shell is hidden under the skin on the back.

Sea hares lay eggs in long, tangled strings attached to seaweed. The larvae that hatch from the eggs drift into deep water where they change to the adult form. Then they move toward the shore, lay their eggs and, soon after, die.

Sea hares are found among the seaweed on which they feed in temperate and warm water along both coasts. A spotted kind grows 4 or 5 inches in length; a tropical kind grows to be a foot long.

BUSHY-BACKED SEA SLUG

Internal shell

←"Ink"

SEA HARE

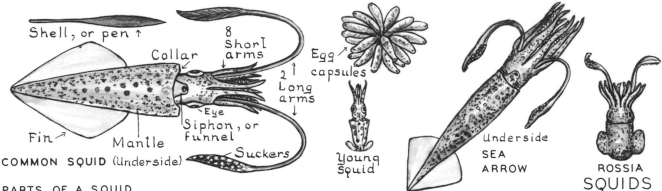

Shell, or pen ↑ · Collar · 8 Short arms · Egg capsules · 2 Long arms · Eye · Siphon, or funnel · Suckers · Fin ↗ · Mantle

COMMON SQUID (Underside)

Young Squid

Underside SEA ARROW

ROSSIA SQUIDS

PARTS OF A SQUID

SQUIDS

The squid is a mollusk whose body is covered by a thick muscular mantle instead of a shell. Its shell is a long "pen" inside of the body. The squid and octopus are classified as cephalopoda which means head-in-the-foot. The foot part of the body is divided into a siphon at the neck and ten arms that surround the head. When the squid feeds, it uses its two long arms to catch the food and pass it to the short arms which hold it against the mouth. The short arms are lined with suckers and the long arms have suckers near the end. The mouth has two horny jaws (the beak) that tear the food apart. Squids eat fishes and other sea life.

A squid travels through the water like a rocket, tail end first. The tail fins wrap around the body, the arms press together and steer. By taking in water around the collar and expelling it through the siphon, the squid moves by jet propulsion. By turning its siphon, it can reverse its direction and travel with the arms and head in front. When it swims slowly it spreads out its tail fins for balance. When the squid is alarmed it shoots from its siphon an inky fluid that clouds the water.

From her siphon the female squid passes her eggs in strings or capsules of jelly. Then with her arms she fastens the jelly containers to seaweed or some other support in the water. After a few weeks the eggs hatch into young that are brightly colored and shaped like the adults.

Squids are used as food, bait, and fertilizer.

Different kinds of small squids are common along all of our coasts. The giant squid, which grows as large as a whale, lives in deep water.

The COMMON SQUID of the temperate Atlantic coast grows to be about 8 inches long. It has triangular fins that extend more than halfway up its body. In color it is dark gray with red or purple spots.

The SEA ARROW is more slender than the common squid and its fins do not extend so far up the body. It can travel backward at great speed. Numbers of these squids may pass through a school of fish striking out in all directions and causing much damage.

ROSSIA SQUIDS, about 3 inches long, have short, rounded bodies and semi-circular fins. In color they are pinkish with brown spots. They are found along the northern and temperate Atlantic coasts.

The RAMSHORN SQUID, which lives in deep water off the Atlantic coast, has a coiled shell at the tail end, most of it inside the body. This white shell, about an inch long, is often found washed up on beaches. The squid has a rather stout body with a rounded tail end. It grows about 3 inches in length and is reddish with brown spots.

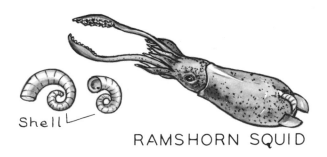

Shell

RAMSHORN SQUID

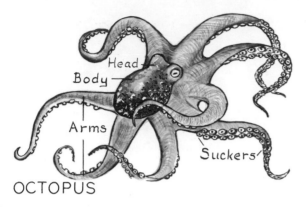

OCTOPUS

OCTOPUSES

An octopus is a mollusk that does not have a shell. Like a squid, it is a head-footed animal. Its foot part is divided into eight arms which are on a wide web around the head. The arms are lined with two rows of suckers which help to anchor the animal to some support. The arms also catch the food and hold it against the hard beak in the mouth which breaks it open. The octopus eats crabs, clams, snails, and a few fishes. Its home, a crevice in the rocks, can often be found by the pile of shells nearby.

The octopus crawls over the bottom on its arms. It can swim backward by jet propulsion, but it is not as fast as a squid. When alarmed it gives off a brown inky fluid from its siphon.

The female lays eggs in jelly capsules which she attaches to a rock or other support. She guards the eggs until they hatch in about two months. The young are shaped like the parents.

The largest octopus does not grow as large as the giant squid. Common Atlantic and Pacific kinds grow from 3 feet or less to 12 feet across including the arms. They are brown, yellow, or reddish, but can change their color to match their surroundings, or when they are excited. They live among rocks in shallow and deep water and are usually harmless.

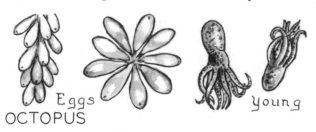

OCTOPUS

COMMON PAPER NAUTILUS

NAUTILUSES

The COMMON PAPER NAUTILUS or ARGONAUT is a relative of the octopus. It does not have a true shell, but the female carries a beautiful, fragile white shell, 4 to 8 inches long, which is the case or cradle that holds the eggs. The female argonaut has six arms around the head and two upper arms which have broad, flat ends. These two arms make and hold the shell. The female grows to be 8 inches or longer. The small male, about 1 inch long, does not have a shell. The argonaut floats in the sea in the warmer waters of the Atlantic and Pacific.

The PEARLY or CHAMBERED NAUTILUS is a primitive cephalopod and belongs to a different group from the octopus. It lives in a shell made by the mantle part of its body. As the animal grows it adds new chambers to the inside of its shell and it lives in the last and largest chamber. Around its head the animal has about ninety tentacles. These capture the small water life that serves as food. Like the squid and octopus, the nautilus swims by shooting water out of its siphon.

The coiled shell is white with wavy brown lines on the outside, pearly on the inside. It grows about 10 inches across. The nautilus lives near the bottom in deep water off the warmer parts of the Pacific coast.

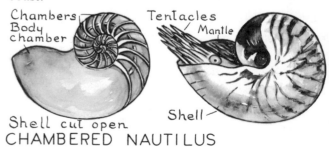

CHAMBERED NAUTILUS

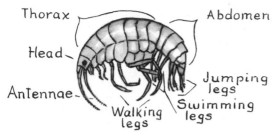

PARTS OF AN AMPHIPOD

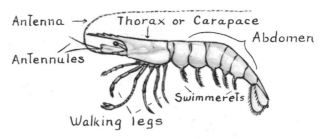

PARTS OF A DECAPOD

SANDHOPPERS AND RELATIVES

Sandhoppers, shrimps, and their relatives belong to the same division of the animal kingdom as the insects; they are Arthropoda or jointed foot animals. They are further classified as crustaceans; their skeleton is a hard crust or shell on the outside of the body. As the animal grows it sheds its old shell by splitting it down the back and wriggling out. The soft, wrinkled skin underneath soon hardens into a new and larger shell. The body of a crustacean, like that of an insect, is usually divided into three sections: head, thorax, and abdomen.

Sandhoppers, scuds, and skeleton shrimp belong to the amphipod group. They have legs for walking, swimming, and jumping. Their body is divided into segments.

SANDHOPPERS (BEACH FLEAS) hop around damp seaweed on the beach. The Atlantic kind is less than ½ inch long; the California variety is 1 inch long.

SCUDS have brownish bodies that are flattened on the sides. They grow to be 1 or 2 inches long. They are found along both the Atlantic and Pacific coasts in shallow water among seaweeds or in deep water.

SKELETON SHRIMP look like part of the seaweed in which they live. They grow ½ to 1 inch in length and are found along the northeastern coast.

SHRIMPS

Shrimps belong to the decapod group of crustaceans. They have ten legs on the thorax. The head and thorax are covered by a single shell (carapace); the abdomen is divided into segments. The abdomen can double up enabling the shrimp to jump as well as swim.

The first two or three pairs of legs have small claws with which the shrimp catches the small sea life that is its food. Under the abdomen are five pairs of swimmerets which aid in swimming and also carry the eggs of the female.

The large kinds of shrimps found in warm waters are used as food. The EDIBLE PRAWN of the Atlantic coast is light brownish and grows 4 to 6 inches long. The BLACK-TAILED SHRIMP found along all of the pacific coast, chiefly in deeper water, is greenish speckled with black and 3 or 4 inches long.

The COMMON PRAWN is found in shallow water among seaweeds along the Atlantic coast. It is translucent with dark specks and about 1¾ inches long.

SNAPPING or PISTOL SHRIMPS, found in warm water along both coasts, have a large claw with which they can make a snapping sound. Of the several kinds, some burrow into the sand, some live in oyster beds, and some live in sponges.

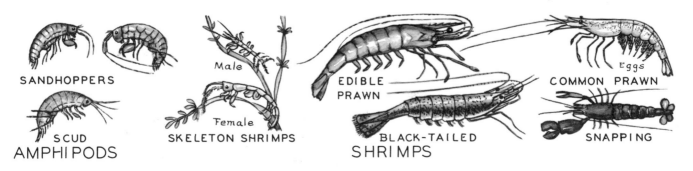

SANDHOPPERS

SCUD

AMPHIPODS

Male

Female

SKELETON SHRIMPS

EDIBLE PRAWN

BLACK-TAILED

SHRIMPS

Eggs

COMMON PRAWN

SNAPPING

AMERICAN LOBSTER

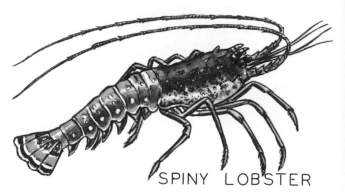

SPINY LOBSTER

AMERICAN LOBSTER

This shellfish (crustacean) is a popular food. The lobster (before cooking) is greenish with darker spots on the upper side, bluish or red on the legs, and yellowish underneath. It grows to 12 or more inches in length and a weight of 1 to 3 pounds or more. A member of the decapod group, it has five pairs of legs. The four back pairs are used for walking and the first pair is developed into large claws. One claw has fine, sharp teeth for catching food, the other has dull, rounded teeth for crushing it. Either claw may be on the left or the right side. Lobsters eat fishes, squids, crabs, and other sea creatures both living and dead, making them useful as scavengers.

When five years old, lobsters are mature and are about 10 inches long. They mate in the spring. From early summer until the following spring, the female carries eggs or developing young attached to her abdominal limbs. After leaving the mother, the young swim about for two months then sink to the bottom to grow into adult lobsters.

Lobsters live in the cooler waters of the Atlantic, in shallow water in summer and deeper water in winter. Many are caught in traps by fishermen.

SPINY LOBSTER OR SEA CRAWFISH

This is another edible crustacean. The meat in the tail end is the part that is eaten. The shell of this crawfish has a varied pattern of brown, red, yellow, and blue. Its five pairs of legs are used for walking; it has no large claws. The long antennae are thick near the head and have an apparatus at their base that can make a grating noise.

The female carries her eggs for over two months. The eggs hatch into spiderlike drifting larvae which later change into the adult form. Found along the southern parts of the Atlantic and Pacific coasts, spiny lobsters are from 8 to 16 inches long.

MANTIS SHRIMP

This crustacean is more like a lobster than a shrimp, but it belongs to a different group from either; it is a stomatopod. It has three pairs of walking legs and one pair of legs that are modified into claws like those of a praying mantis.

Mantis shrimps grow from 3 to 6 or sometimes 12 inches long. The kind that is found along the Atlantic coast is greenish with some yellow and pink. The California variety is blue and orange.

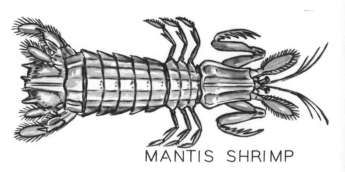

MANTIS SHRIMP

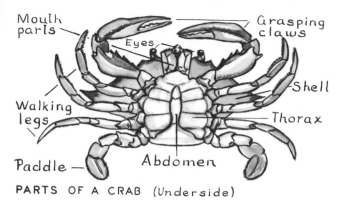

PARTS OF A CRAB (Underside)

BLUE CRAB

CRABS

A crab is a crustacean of the decapod group. It has five pairs of legs, the first pair modified into grasping claws. In the swimming crabs, the last pair of legs usually has a broad paddle at the end. A crab travels sideways on its walking legs. If a leg is lost a new one grows in. The crab's eyes are on movable stalks and can be raised to look in any direction. The largest part of a crab's body is the thorax which is covered on the back by a broad carapace, or shell. The small, narrow abdomen bends under the body where it fits into a groove.

A crab grabs its food with its large claws and carries it to its mouth where it is torn up by the movable parts around the mouth. Crabs are scavengers; they eat any kind of animal food, living or dead.

In summer female crabs have one or two sets of eggs which they carry under their tail end until they hatch. The larvae swim about and go through several stages before changing to the adult form. As the young crabs grow they shed their shells and form new ones. Small kinds of crabs live for two or three years; large kinds may live to ten years.

Different kinds of crabs are found along all of our shores.

Larva developing into young crab

LIFE HISTORY OF A CRAB

SWIMMING CRABS

The BLUE CRAB is the common edible crab of the Atlantic and Gulf coasts. It is olive-brown or dark green on the back; its legs are tinted with bright blue and have some red marks. Its shell grows to 6 inches across and has a sharp spine on either side. As the crab grows it sheds its old, hard shell and forms a new one that is soft at first. In this state it is sold as a soft-shell crab. Blue crabs live in brackish water near the mouths of rivers in summer and move into deeper water in winter.

The LADY or CALICO CRAB makes a burrow in the sand where it sits with its large claws thrust out. It has a nearly circular shell that grows to be 3 inches across. The shell is light colored and has an all-over pattern of purple or red spots.

The GREEN CRAB grows to be 3 inches across. It is olive-green or brownish with a pattern of bright green on the back. Young crabs are green with black dots and markings on the back. The last pair of legs, instead of being paddle-shaped are flat and bordered with hairs. The green crab and the lady crab are found along the Atlantic coast.

LADY   GREEN

CRABS

COMMON ROCK CRAB

ROCK AND MUD CRABS

These crabs have legs that are adapted to walking rather than swimming.

Rock crabs live along rocky shores, on sandy bottoms, and in tide pools. Their circular or oval shells have rounded indentations across the front and sharper ones on the sides.

The BIG CRAB or MARKET CRAB is the edible crab of the Pacific coast. Its reddish-brown shell grows to over a foot across.

The COMMON ROCK CRAB of the Atlantic coast has a yellowish shell closely dotted with reddish-brown. The JONAH CRAB of the northern Atlantic coast is brownish-red shading to yellowish. These two crabs grow to be 3 or 4 inches across.

Mud crabs have a broad, brownish shell. They live on muddy bottoms, often where there are oyster or other shells and stones. Some small kinds found along the Atlantic coast have a black tip on their large claws.

The STONE CRAB is found along the southern Atlantic coast where it burrows into the sand. It is a stout crab with a hard, purplish or brownish-red shell. It grows 5 inches across and is good to eat.

PACIFIC   ATLANTIC   GHOST CRAB

MOLE CRABS

SAND CRABS

These crabs live on moist, sandy beaches.

MOLE CRABS or SAND BUGS burrow into sand at the edge of the water moving with the tide to keep ahead of the waves. They have short, broad, flat legs that are adapted to digging. Most of their body is covered by a curved shell. The tail end curls underneath. Two featherlike antennae stick up above the sand and catch the organic matter that is their food. The Pacific mole crab has a brown shell about an inch long. The Atlantic crab has a light yellowish shell about 1½ inches long.

GHOST or SAND CRABS are small crabs that burrow into the sand at the edge of the high tide mark. When they move about they go sideways swiftly. When they stop they seem to disappear because they are the same color as the sand. They are more active at night. These crabs are found along the warmer parts of the Atlantic coast.

FIDDLER CRABS are found on beaches and salt marshes on both coasts where they make long burrows in the sand. Their squarish, light or dark brown shell is about an inch long. The male crab has one large claw which he uses to court the female and to fight other males. Ghost and fiddler crabs eat tiny animal and plant life in the sand.

MUD CRAB

STONE CRAB

Female   Male

FIDDLER CRABS

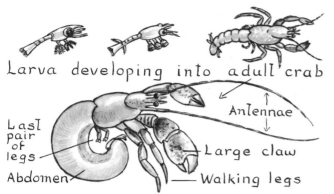

LIFE HISTORY AND PARTS OF A HERMIT CRAB

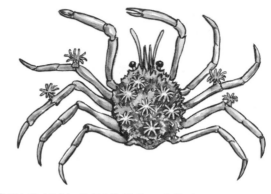

COMMON SPIDER CRAB

HERMIT CRAB

This crab has a soft body without a shell. For protection it carries the shell of a sea snail on its back end. The crab's abdomen is curved so that it fits into the shell. Hooks on its lower end and its last two pairs of legs help to hold the shell in place. With two pairs of walking legs and two large claws sticking out of the shell the crab pulls itself around. In its claws it catches and breaks up the flesh food that it eats.

Early in spring the female crab has clusters of eggs which cling to her body inside the shell. The eggs hatch into larvae which have first a swimming stage, then one in which they resemble tiny crawfish. After this they molt and develop a curved abdomen. Then they have to find a small shell to cover them. As the crab grows it moves into larger shells.

Different kinds of hermit crabs grow from 1 to 3 inches long. The smaller ones use periwinkle, mud, and moon snail shells; the larger ones use turban, tulip, and whelk shells. These crabs live in tide pools and shallow water on all of our coasts.

SPIDER CRABS

These crabs have rather pear-shaped bodies with the head at the narrow end. They have five pairs of long legs, the first pair modified into slender claws. Many of these crabs pick up algae, small animal life, and other debris with their claws and place it on their backs as a kind of camouflage. When the crab molts, these trimmings are discarded with the shell.

The crab in the picture at the top of the page has tiny sea anemones on its back and legs. This is the COMMON SPIDER CRAB found in shallow water over muddy bottoms and on seaweed along the Atlantic coast. It is mud-colored and grows to be about 2½ inches long.

The GREEN SPIDER CRAB has a small body that is narrow in front and very long slender legs. It is found on the southern Atlantic coast.

The TOAD CRAB has a squat, toad-shaped, reddish-brown body and moderately long legs. It grows about 3 inches long and is found along the Atlantic coast, most commonly in the northern part, in shallow water with a muddy or stony bottom.

HERMIT CRABS

TOAD   GREEN
SPIDER CRABS

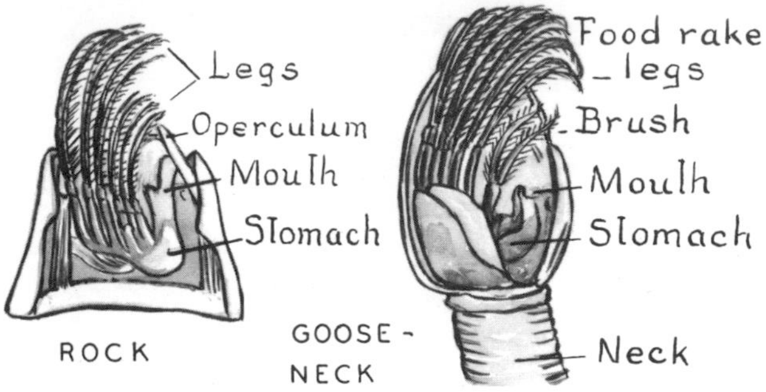
Legs
Operculum
Mouth
Stomach
Food rake legs
Brush
Mouth
Stomach
Neck
ROCK
GOOSE-NECK

PARTS OF A BARNACLE

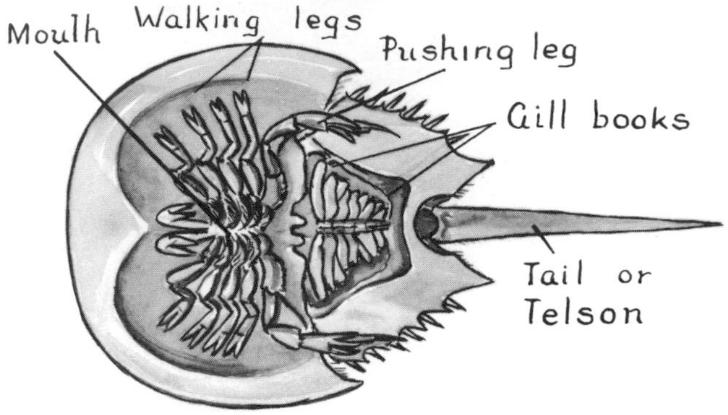
Mouth
Walking legs
Pushing leg
Gill books
Tail or Telson

PARTS OF A HORSESHOE CRAB

BARNACLES

The barnacle is a crustacean that has a very different shape from its relatives, the shrimps, crabs, and lobsters. The ROCK BARNACLE is covered by a cone-shaped shell that is made of six heavy plates joined by thinner pieces of shell. An opening in the top of the shell has a door (operculum) made of four small pieces of shell. The door closes when the barnacle is alarmed or exposed to air at low tide.

Inside the shell the barnacle lies on its back and sticks its legs out of the top opening. The legs wave in the water and collect the small organic matter that serves as food.

Barnacles lay eggs that are held inside the shell. The eggs hatch into larvae which swim away. The larvae go through several changes then settle down on some support and develop into the adult form. Barnacles cement themselves to one spot where they remain. They are found along all coasts.

Different kinds of ROCK BARNACLES have grayish, creamy, or pink shells from ¼ to 2 inches long.

GOOSENECK BARNACLES have a five-pieced shell at the end of a rubbery stalk, or neck, that is attached to some support. The shell grows from 1 to 2 inches and the stalk from ½ to 12 inches long.

HORSESHOE OR KING CRAB

This creature is not related to the edible king crab of the Pacific, or to any of the other crabs. It is a primitive form related to scorpions and spiders. Its back is covered by a broad brown shell that has two parts with a hinge between. As the crab grows it splits its shell along the front edge and squeezes out. Cast-off shells often float ashore.

The horseshoe crab uses its first four pairs of legs for walking and the fifth pair for swimming or pushing through sand or mud. It sticks its tail in the sand to help turn itself over. The crab eats small animal life that it finds in the sand and mud.

The female is larger than the male. She may grow to be 20 inches long. In early summer she lays eggs in a hollow that she digs in sand near the shore. The eggs hatch in mid-summer into young that are shaped like the adults but lack a tail. Horseshoe crabs are found in shallow water all along our eastern coast.

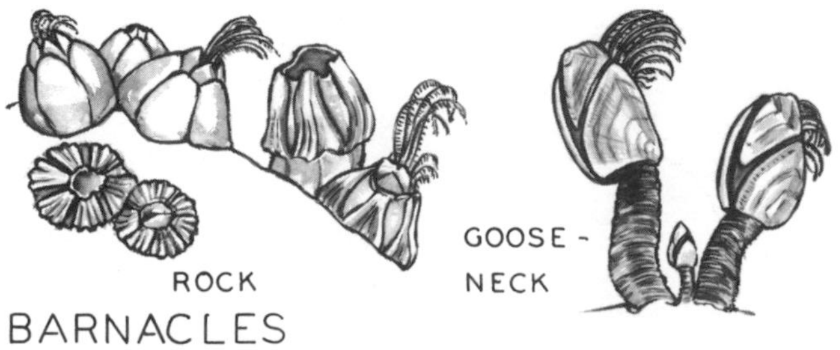
ROCK
GOOSE-NECK

BARNACLES

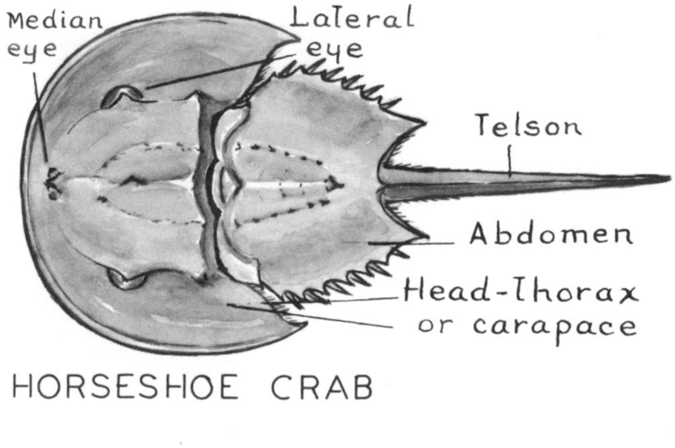
Median eye
Lateral eye
Telson
Abdomen
Head-Thorax or carapace

HORSESHOE CRAB

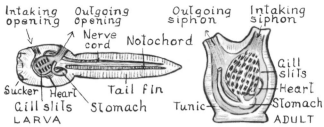

PARTS OF A SEA SQUIRT

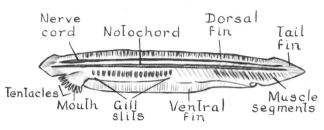

PARTS OF A LANCELET

SEA SQUIRTS: TUNICATA

Sea squirts look like simple blobs of jelly, but they belong to the highest order of animals, Chordata, because in the larval form they have a notochord which is the forerunner of a backbone.

The tiny larva which comes from a sea squirt egg is shaped like a tadpole complete with a tail which enables it to swim. In the tail are a nerve cord and a notochord. As the larva develops it settles head down on some object and becomes attached. The tail, with the notochord, then disappears leaving only the body part to become the adult sea squirt.

The adult's body has a tough jelly-like skin or tunic with two openings or siphons, one to take water in and the other to squirt it out. Water passes through the gill slits to furnish oxygen for breathing and small particles of food. Adult sea squirts multiply by budding new individuals from the side of old ones as well as by producing eggs. Sea squirts live on rocks, seaweed, sand, and wood. Different kinds are found along both coasts.

SEA VASES are transparent and about 1½ inches high. SEA GRAPES are yellowish, about an inch across and grow in clusters. SEA PEACHES are about the size, shape, and color of a peach. SEA PORK is a low-growing, yellowish or pinkish, jelly-like mass.

LANCELET: AMPHIOXUS

The common name of this animal is derived from its lance-shaped tail. Amphioxus means sharp at both ends. The lancelet is a simple fishlike creature which has a nerve cord and a notochord in place of a backbone running from the front of its head to the tip of its tail.

The lancelet has a transparent body which is flattened from side to side. It has a fin along the back and underneath. Most of the time it lives in a burrow in the sand with its head end out. The mouth opening is surrounded by a hood that has a fringe of tentacles. Water entering the mouth passes over the gill slits where small particles are strained out to be used as food.

Sometimes the lancelet comes out of its burrow to swim about. If alarmed it dives into the sand and disappears in a flash. Lancelets breed at night in early summer. They produce eggs which hatch into swimming larvae. The larvae develop into adults and make burrows.

Lancelets are found in sand under shallow or deeper water along both coasts in the more southerly parts. The VIRGINIA LANCELET grows to about 2 inches in length and the CALIFORNIA LANCELET to 3 inches.

SEA SQUIRTS

LANCELET

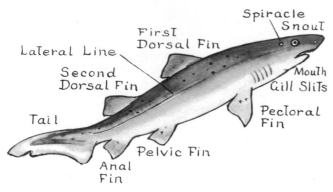

SAND SHARK

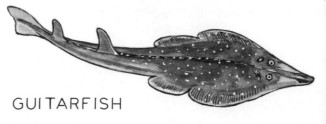

GUITARFISH

SHARKS

Sharks are primitive fishes. Their backbone is not true bone, but is cartilage hardened by lime.

The shark has a snout with the mouth underneath. Two spiracles on top of the head permit water to enter and five to seven gill slits on each side let the water out. The shark's body does not have scales like those of bony fishes, but it has small teethlike scales scattered through the skin. The teeth in the mouth are modified scales that are replaced as they wear down.

A shark is near-sighted; its senses of smell and vibration help it to find its food. It eats fishes and other animal life, usually slow or disabled creatures as it is not able to swim very fast. Its body fins are not very flexible and it uses the tail fin for swimming. Since the shark has no swim bladder to keep it afloat, it must move about to keep from sinking.

Some kinds of sharks lay eggs; some kinds hatch the eggs inside the female's body; other kinds bear the young alive. Many different kinds of sharks are found in warm and temperate waters along both of our coasts. They range in size from 2 to 50 feet long. The whale shark is the largest of all fishes.

RAYS

The ray, like the shark, has a backbone of cartilage instead of true bone. It looks something like a shark that has been flattened out. The eyes, with the spiracles behind them, are on the top of the head and the mouth and gill slits are underneath. The pectoral fins are wide and continuous with the head. The tail is often long and very thin.

GUITAR FISHES come between sharks and rays. The tail end resembles a shark and the head end resembles a ray. The guitar fish uses its tail for swimming and its pectoral fins for steering. The spotted guitar fish of the East Coast grows to about 2 feet in length. The West Coast species grows to be 4 feet long. Both kinds live in shallow warm water where they swim near the bottom or half bury themselves in sand. They feed on mollusks and crustaceans.

The SAWFISH is a ray which has the general shape of a shark, execpt for its snout which is long, narrow, and flat, and has teeth on each side like a saw. It uses the saw in defense, and also to poke around the bottom to find the crustaceans, and to catch the small fishes that it eats.

The sawfish bears its young alive. The young are 2 feet long. Adults grow to be 20 feet long. They live near the bottom in warm shallow water off the Atlantic and Gulf coasts.

SAWFISH

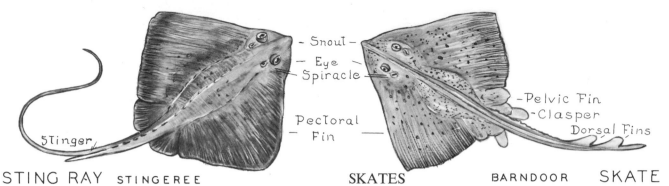

STING RAY STINGEREE

SKATES BARNDOOR SKATE

STING RAYS

Sting rays have flattened bodies and wide pectoral fins that look like wings. Most kinds have thin tails with one or more poisonous spines which can inflict painful wounds. These rays swim over reefs and sandy bottoms in shallow, warm water searching for crustaceans, mollusks, and fishes to eat. Sometimes they partly bury themselves in the sand. The females carry the eggs in their bodies until they hatch, then bear the young alive.

The STINGEREE has a long, whiplike tail with a poison spine near its base. One kind, found in the southern Atlantic, grows to be 15 inches across. Another kind, found as far north as Cape Cod, grows to be 5 feet across.

BUTTERFLY RAYS, which are found along our southern Atlantic coast, have very wide fins and short, thin tails. One kind that grows to be 2 feet across does not have a stinger. Another kind grows to be 7 feet across and does have a stinger.

ROUND STING RAYS, found off the southern Atlantic and California coasts, grow about 2 feet long.

A skate has a backbone of cartilage. It has wing-like pectoral fins which move in undulating or flapping motions enabling the skate to swim. Its long tail with two small fins near the end is used for steering. The tail does not have a stinger.

Skates lay eggs in dark colored cases which have two prongs at each end. Threads fastened to the prongs at one end anchor the case to some support under water. Each case usually contains only one egg. The egg hatches in some species after from four to six months, in other species it may take much longer. The young skate emerges from the free end of the case with its winglike fins folded over its body. The egg cases are sometimes washed up on beaches and are called sea purses. Skates are mottled brownish on the back to match the sea bottom and light underneath. They live in shallow water where they hunt for crustaceans and fishes to eat. Sometimes they hide in the sand with only their eyes showing.

The CLEARNOSE SKATE lives along most of the Atlantic coast and grows to be 2 feet long. The COMMON SKATE grows to 2 feet and the BARNDOOR SKATE to be 3 feet in length. Both are found in the northern Atlantic. On the Pacific coast, the CALIFORNIA SKATE grows to be 2½ feet long; the BIG SKATE grows from 6 to 8 feet long.

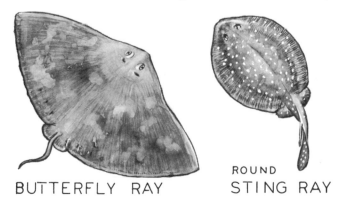

BUTTERFLY RAY

ROUND STING RAY

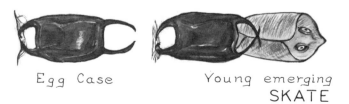

Egg Case

Young emerging SKATE

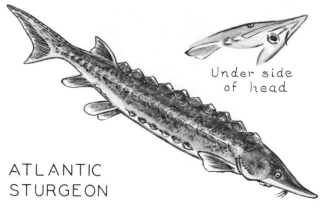

ATLANTIC
STURGEON

PRIMITIVE BONY FISHES

STURGEONS have a backbone made of cartilage, but they also have a row of large, bony plates along the back and two rows of smaller plates along each side. The sturgeon has a long snout with mouth and barbels underneath. As it swims over the bottom the barbels feel small creatures in the mud, then the tubular, toothless mouth shoots out to suck them in.

The ATLANTIC STURGEON grows to 12 feet in length and the SHORT-NOSED STURGEON, also of the Atlantic, to 3 feet. In spring sturgeons go up rivers to lay their eggs. The flesh of these fishes is good to eat and the eggs (roe) are sold as caviar.

GARS have long, slender bodies covered with diamond-shaped scales that are coated with an enamel-like substance. Their scaly skin and the separate scales are used in making jewelry.

Gars catch many other fishes with their long jaws and sharp teeth. They live mostly in warm fresh water, but sometimes go into the brackish water of bays along our southern Atlantic coast and the Gulf of Mexico.

Since their swim bladder also serves as a lung, they often come to the surface to take in air. Gars grow 5 to 10 feet in length.

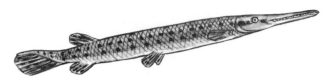

LONGNOSE GAR

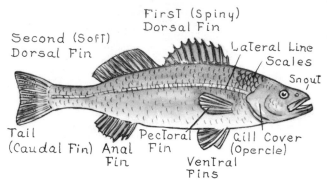

PARTS OF A BONY FISH

BONY FISHES

Most of the fishes of the sea have bony skeletons. Their fins have bony rays which make them flexible and more useful for swimming. A swim bladder (a gas-filled sac) helps the fish to float. Some fishes make noises by vibrating the muscles around the swim bladder.

Bony fishes are many different shapes, sizes, and colors. Their color may change to match their surroundings, and the immature fishes may be a different color from the adults. Most fishes have scales on their bodies, but some do not. All have a single pair of gill openings, usually with a wide, horny cover. Most fishes are near-sighted, but have a lateral line that can sense vibrations. Some fishes have barbels around the mouth that have a sense of taste. Most kinds have teeth, but some do not.

Some fishes eat other animals, some eat plants. Those that have a mouth toward the upper side usually feed near the surface; those with the mouth on the under side feed on the bottom.

Most of the bony fishes of the sea lay large numbers of eggs that float about. The large numbers are necessary since many eggs and young are devoured by other creatures. Some kinds of fishes make nests and guard their young. They do not lay as many eggs since their young have a better chance to grow up. Fish eggs hatch into larvae that are somewhat like tiny tadpoles. The larvae soon grow fins and take on the shape of the adult fish. Some kinds of fishes bear their young alive.

CALIFORNIA
SARDINE

ATLANTIC
HERRING

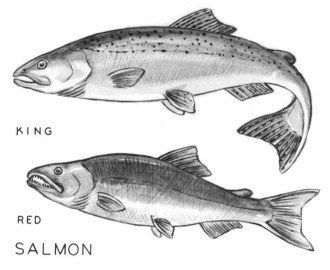

KING

RED

SALMON

HERRINGS

The herring family is one of the oldest and most abundant of the bony fishes. Herrings can be told by their forked tail fin, short dorsal fin without spines, lack of a lateral line, medium or small size, and usually silver and bluish coloring.

Herrings travel in gigantic schools made up of thousands of individuals, usually near the surface out at sea; young fishes usually stay close to shore. They feed largely on plankton (small, floating sea life). Sardines are members of the herring family.

CALIFORNIA SARDINES, or PILCHARDS, are caught in great numbers. They are used in canning, for industrial products, and young ones are used for bait. Adults grow about 10 inches long.

COMMON ATLANTIC HERRINGS are canned as sardines when they are small. Adults grow to 14 inches in length. They live in cold water. In autumn they move toward the shore to lay their eggs.

The MENHADEN grows about a foot in length. It is common along the Atlantic coast, in the northern part in summer and the southern part in winter. It is not a food fish, but is used to furnish oil, fish meal for animals, and fertilizer.

SALMON

Salmon are large fishes that live in the northern Pacific. At breeding time in spring or summer they go up rivers along our northwestern coast to lay their eggs and die. The young fish remain in fresh water for a few weeks or years, depending on the species, before they swim out to sea.

Salmon have rather large heads and at breeding time the males have hooked jaws. All have a long anal fin and a small fatty fin opposite it on the back. Their color is silvery, sometimes overlaid with shades of red, blue, or green. Great numbers of salmon are used in the canning industry.

The ATLANTIC SALMON is a large trout that lives in cold sea waters except at breeding time in spring or fall, when it goes up rivers along our northeastern coast. It does not necessarily die after laying its eggs and may breed more than once. This fish is silvery with a brownish back and X-shaped black spots. It may weigh 15 pounds or more.

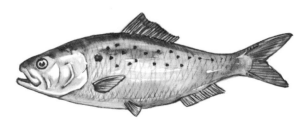

MENHADEN

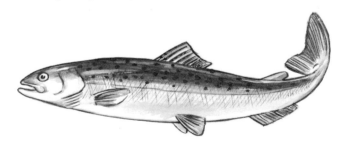

ATLANTIC SALMON

SMELT

SMELTS have a silvery stripe along the lateral line and grow to about 8 inches in length. They swim in large schools in cool water along the Atlantic coast except in late winter and early spring when they go up rivers and streams to breed. The WHITE-BAIT SMELT of the Pacific coast is similar.

GRUNION

The CALIFORNIA GRUNION grows to 6 or 8 inches long. It has a silver stripe along the side, but no lateral line. In spring and summer, at the highest tide of the month, grunions go to beaches and lay their eggs in the sand. At the next highest tide, a month later, the eggs hatch and the young swim out.

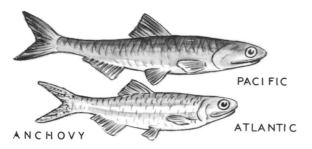

PACIFIC

ATLANTIC

ANCHOVY

ANCHOVIES are found in both the Atlantic and Pacific. They swim in schools near the surface and feed on plankton. The anchovy has a large mouth, large scales, and a forked tail. The ATLANTIC BAY ANCHOVY has a silver stripe and grows 3 or 4 inches long. The PACIFIC ANCHOVY grows to 9 inches.

STRIPED MULLET

MULLETS swim in schools in warm, shallow water along the Atlantic and Pacific coasts. They feed on small plant and animal life that they find on the muddy bottom. The STRIPED MULLET is silvery with narrow, dark, horizontal stripes on the upper side. It grows from 1 to 2 feet in length.

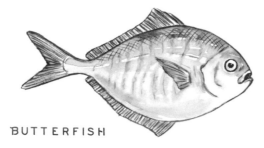

BUTTERFISH

BUTTERFISH swim in schools over sandy bottoms in warm water along the Atlantic coast, where they feed on plankton. They have silvery, round, flattened bodies 6 to 9 inches long. The HARVESTFISH is similar and lives in more southern waters. The CALIFORNIA POMPANO is a Pacific harvestfish.

BLACKFISH

The BLACKFISH or TAUTOG has a white chin and an olive or brownish body with black blotches. It grows about 2 feet long. In summer it is found off New England around rocks and piers where it feeds on mussels and other small mollusks and crustaceans. Winters, it moves south or into deeper water.

SCUP or PORGY

The NORTHERN SCUP OR PORGY grows about 10 inches long. It is dusky on the back and fins and has bright silver patches on the sides. Scup travel in schools and feed on the bottom along the New England coast in summer. In winter they go into deeper water. A similar species lives in southern waters.

WHITING or KINGFISH

The WHITING OR KINGFISH grows about 17 inches long. It is grayish with darker blotches on the back, light underneath. It has a barbel under the chin and a high, spiny dorsal fin. Whiting travel in schools off the northern Atlantic coast. Similar species are found off the southern parts of both coasts.

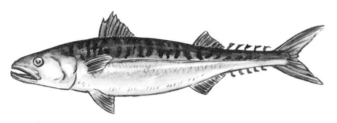

MACKEREL

The MACKEREL grows to 1 or 1½ feet in length. It is bluish-green with dark markings on the back and silvery on the sides. Mackerel swim in huge schools. They appear off our northern Atlantic coast in spring and summer. In fall they move southward. A somewhat similar species lives in the Pacific.

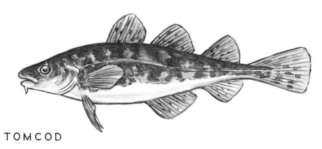

TOMCOD

The TOMCOD is a small (about 15 inches long) member of the cod family. It is olive or grayish on the back and yellow or white underneath. The back and fins are mottled. Tomcod live close to shore in cool water. One kind lives along the northern Atlantic coast and another kind along the Pacific.

SEA BASS

The SEA BASS grows to be 18 inches long. It is gray on the back with darker markings and has white spots on the scales. The dorsal fins are black and white. The tail fin has a long ray at the top. Sea bass are found around wrecks, rocks, or pilings along the Atlantic coast.

WEAKFISH

The WEAKFISH grows to 16 inches or longer. It is olive with dark, spotty lines on the back, silvery on the sides; the lower fins are yellow or gray. Weakfish are found along the Atlantic coast, often in large schools. They swim in shallow water in warm weather and deeper water in winter.

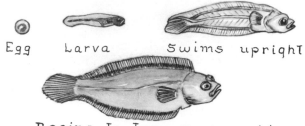

Egg   Larva   Swims upright

Begins to turn on one side
YOUNG WINTER FLOUNDER

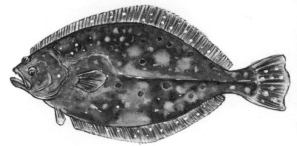

SUMMER FLOUNDER or FLUKE

FLATFISHES

Because of their flattened bodies and their habit of swimming on one side, these fishes are able to live in shallow water where they sometimes partly bury themselves in the sandy or muddy bottom. The upper side of the body is darker in color and often mottled to match the bottom sand; the under side is light. The two eyes are on the upper side, but the mouth is on both sides.

Young flatfishes are upright at first like other fishes and have one eye on each side. As they grow larger they begin to swim on one side and one eye moves either to the right or the left, whichever is the upper side; some kinds face to the left, others to the right. Flatfishes have sharp teeth; they feed on minnows, soft crabs, worms, squids, and mollusks.

Most flatfishes are fairly easy to catch, and they are good eating.

The COMMON or WINTER FLOUNDER is found along the Atlantic coast in winter and early spring,

the time when it lays its eggs. In summer it goes into deeper water. This fish grows from 12 to 30 inches in length. It is olive-green, brownish, or black on the back, sometimes with darker spots.

The SUMMER or NORTHERN FLOUNDER or FLUKE, is found along the Atlantic shore from Cape Cod southward in summer; in winter it goes into deeper water. These fish grow to a length of 2 to 3 feet. They vary in color to match their surroundings; some have dark spots on the back. This flounder faces toward the left.

The ATLANTIC and PACIFIC HALIBUTS are the largest of the flatfishes and are important food fish. They may grow to 8 feet in length and 300 pounds in weight. They are dark brown or light brown with dark rings on the back and are caught in fairly deep water offshore in northern, but not very cold water. The CALIFORNIA HALIBUT, caught in spring from San Francisco southward, is smaller. It grows to 3 feet in length and 60 pounds in weight.

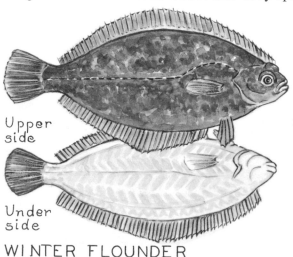

Upper side

Under side

WINTER FLOUNDER

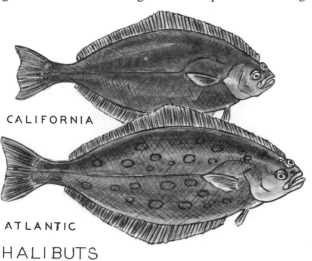

CALIFORNIA

ATLANTIC

HALIBUTS

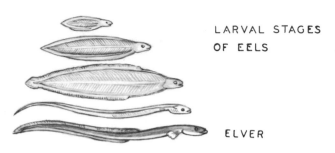

LARVAL STAGES
OF EELS

ELVER

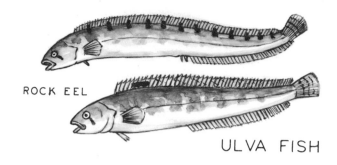

ROCK EEL

ULVA FISH

EELS

An eel has a long, snakelike body with a long fin that goes around the tail end. It is dark on the back and light underneath. It has a large mouth and short, strong teeth; it eats almost any kind of animal food and some water plants. Eels grow to be 4 or 5 feet long, the females being the longer.

Eels live in fresh or brackish water near the Atlantic coast until they are from 7 to 15 years old and are ready to breed. Then, in summer or fall, they start on their last journey. They swim along the Atlantic coast and southeastward all the way to the Sargasso Sea. There each female lays her tiny eggs, several million of them. This great number is needed since the larvae that hatch from the eggs have to make the long and perilous journey to the Atlantic coast. The larvae are small, transparent, leaf-shaped creatures that live on plankton. When they reach the coast, after about a year, they are 2 or 3 inches long, slender and dark in color. At this stage they are called elvers. Now they enter the mouths of rivers. The females travel far up the rivers and into lakes. The males usually stay in brackish water near the coast.

EEL-LIKE FISHES

In northern Atlantic waters are several kinds of fishes that are eel-like in their general shape and arrangement of fins although they are stouter in the body.

The ROCK EEL, which lives in crevices along the shore, varies in color from olive-brown to light red on the back and is yellowish underneath. It has a row of dark spots on the back. It is from 6 to 12 inches long.

The ULVA FISH lives among seaweed and under stones near the low-tide mark and in deeper water. It grows to be 6 inches long and is brownish on the back with an oval blotch on the dorsal fin.

The RETICULATED EELPOUT lives along the shore on the bottom where it grows to 15 inches or longer. It is brownish on the back with irregular dark lines and has a dark edge on the dorsal fin.

The SHORE EELPOUT lives on the bottom in shallow and deeper water. In color it is yellowish or reddish-brown with darker markings on the back. It grows to 2½ feet in length, 3 pounds or more in weight, and is sometimes used as a food fish.

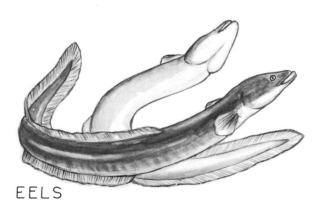

EELS

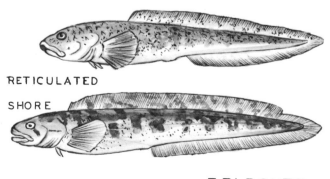

RETICULATED

SHORE

EELPOUTS

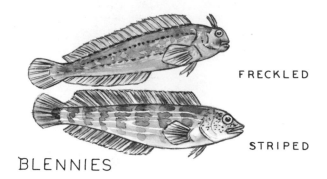

FRECKLED

STRIPED

BLENNIES

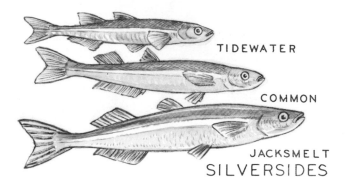

TIDEWATER

COMMON

JACKSMELT

SILVERSIDES

BLENNIES AND GOBIES

Blennies are small fishes that are found in tide pools and shallow water along all of our coasts. The FRECKLED BLENNY is brownish or greenish and grows to be 3 inches long. It is found along the southern Atlantic and Gulf coasts. The STRIPED BLENNY grows to 5 inches in length and is mottled in color to match the seaweed among which it lives. It is found along the Atlantic coast north to New York. Other blennies are found along the Pacific coast.

Gobies are small fishes that live in warm, shallow water. The NAKED GOBY, so called because it does not have scales, is common in southern bays and sometimes is found as far north as Cape Cod. It often lurks in empty shells. It grows to be 3 inches long and is grayish with dark blotches on the back. The LONGJAW GOBY is a Pacific species that grows 3 or 4 inches in length. It is greenish and brownish in color. The SLEEPER is a southern Atlantic goby that grows to a foot in length. Its markings vary.

SILVERSIDES AND KILLIFISHES

Silversides are slender fishes that swim in schools near the shore. They are dark on the back, silvery underneath and have a bright silver stripe along the sides. The TIDEWATER SILVERSIDE, which grows to 3 inches in length, and the COMMON SILVERSIDE, which grows to be 6 inches long, are found along the Atlantic coast. The JACKSMELT is a silverside found along the Pacific coast. It grows to from 10 to 22 inches and is an important food fish.

Killifishes live in weedy waters close to shore along the Atlantic coast. They grow to be 5 or 6 inches long. The COMMON KILLIFISH or MUMMY-CHOG is bluish or greenish with dark bars on the back and yellow underneath. Another kind has white and yellow spots on the sides. Both are used for bait. The BROAD or VARIEGATED KILLIFISH grows to be 3 inches long and is bluish gray with darker spots on the back. In spring and summer the males are orange underneath and have flashes of blue on the sides.

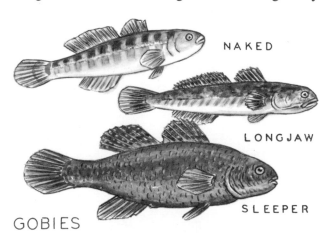

NAKED

LONGJAW

SLEEPER

GOBIES

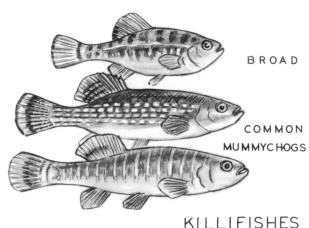

BROAD

COMMON

MUMMYCHOGS

KILLIFISHES

TEN-SPINED STICKLEBACK

STICKLEBACKS

These little fish have spines on their backs in front of the dorsal fin. Different kinds have two, three, four, five, or ten spines. All, except the five-spined which lives in brooks, live in salt or brackish water in marshes and shallow coastal areas. Those that live along the northern Atlantic coast usually go up rivers and creeks in spring to breed. The males go first. They are smaller than the females and are dark on the back; yellow, orange, or rosy-red on the sides.

The male fish makes a nest from bits of water weed fastened together with a threadlike mucus that he secretes. Some kinds of sticklebacks build on the bottom, others attach their nests to plant stems. After the nest is made, the male drives a female into it. She lays her eggs, then leaves them for the male to guard until they hatch, usually in about a week.

The TEN-SPINED STICKLEBACK grows to 3 inches in length and is olive-green with dark bars on the back, silvery underneath.

The FOUR-SPINED STICKLEBACK female grows to be 2½ inches long and the male to 1½ inches. He is olive or brown on the back, silver and yellow underneath.

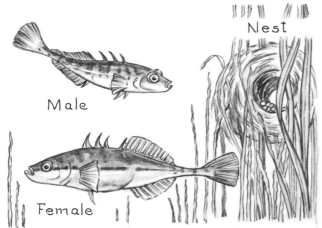

Male

Nest

Female

FOUR-SPINED STICKLEBACKS

Young

Female

Male

SEA HORSES

SEA HORSES AND PIPEFISHES

These two fishes are covered with thin, bony plates made of small scales joined together. The male has a pouch on the front part of the tail, where it joins the body, in which the female lays her eggs. The eggs stay in the pouch until they hatch.

SEA HORSES have a long snout and earlike pectoral fins. They have a fan-shaped dorsal fin that waves very fast when they swim. The long, flexible tail can be coiled around seaweed. In this position seahorses feed, reaching out to catch small crustaceans that swim by. The adult fish are always upright, but the newly hatched swim horizontally.

Sea horses are found along our Atlantic coast and off Mexico in the Pacific. They vary in length from 2 to 12 inches depending on the species.

PIPEFISHES are found in the same places as sea horses although some kinds are more common farther north. Pipefishes have slender bodies and a tail fin as well as a dorsal fin. They swim with their dorsal fins and by waving their bodies like eels. They are silvery underneath, green or brown on the back to match the eelgrass or seaweeds among which they live. Different kinds grow from 4 to 12 inches in length.

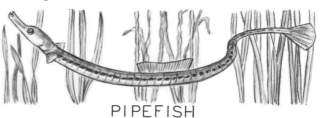

PIPEFISH

COMMON TRUNKFISH

COMMON FILEFISH

COWFISH

ORANGE FILEFISH

TRUNKFISHES AND FILEFISHES

Trunkfishes have a body encased in a shell made of 6-sided scales fused together. They move about slowly with the help of their dorsal and anal fins. The pectoral fins help circulate water through the gills. The mouth is small; the teeth are fused together in the form of a beak. Trunkfishes are found in warm water along the Atlantic coast. They feed on small plant and animal life.

The COMMON TRUNKFISH, which grows to 10 inches in length, has a rough mottled shell.

The COWFISH grows to be a foot long. Its shell has iridescent blue and yellow spots.

Filefishes receive their name from their tough skin which has small, hard scales embedded in it. The skin formerly was used like sandpaper. These fishes have a spine over the eyes and a deep ventral flap. The dorsal and anal fins are used for swimming. With its small mouth, which has sharp teeth, the fish grazes on plant and animal material around pilings. Filefishes live in warm Atlantic waters.

The COMMON FILEFISH grows 10 inches long and is green, brown, or gray to match its surroundings.

The ORANGE FILEFISH is mottled orange or brown with dark spots. It grows to be 1 or 2 feet long.

INFLATED FISHES

PUFFERS or SWELLFISHES, when they are disturbed, inflate their bodies with air or water until they are almost round. In this state they may float on their backs at the surface. Instead of scales on their body, they have spines. They have a small mouth with four large teeth which are used to crush the mollusks and shellfishes that they eat.

Puffers live along the Atlantic coast. The NORTHERN PUFFER grows to 10 inches long and is mottled, dark greenish on the back, light underneath.

The SMOOTH PUFFER lives in warm waters. It is 2 feet long and is mottled grayish on the back.

The BURFISH or BOXFISH has short, stout spines over its body. It is 10 inches long and is olive or brownish with dark, wavy stripes and spots on the back, yellowish underneath. Its teeth are fused into a beak. The skin of this fish is sometimes used to make lanterns.

The PORCUPINE FISH grows from 1 to 3 feet long. It is brownish and has long, stout spines that stand out in all directions when the body is inflated.

The burfish and the porcupine fish do not inflate as readily as the puffers. They live in shallow warm water, but sometimes as far north as Cape Cod.

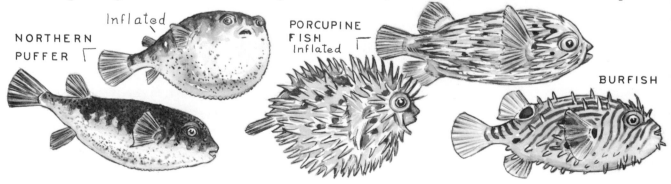

NORTHERN PUFFER

Inflated

PORCUPINE FISH Inflated

BURFISH

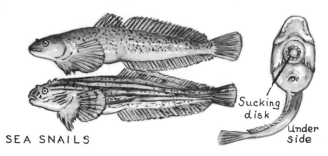

SEA SNAILS

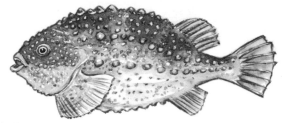

LUMPFISH

SEA SNAILS have smooth skins. Their ventral fins are modified to form a sucking disk with which they cling. One kind is brownish with light and dark marks and dots; another is red, green, yellow, or lilac with dark stripes. Both grow 4 to 6 inches long and live along rocky shores of the northern Atlantic.

Young LUMPFISH resemble sea snails to which they are related. Adult lumpfish have stocky bodies covered with large and small lumps. They grow to a length of 20 inches and are varied in color, the males being brighter than the females. Lumpfish live along rocky northeastern shores.

LONGHORN SCULPIN

LIONFISH

SCULPINS have spiny heads and large, fanlike, pectoral fins. The LONGHORN SCULPIN is olive or brownish with light and dark blotches that vary to match its surroundings. It grows to 18 inches long and is found in the northern Atlantic in deep water in summer, near shore in winter.

The LIONFISH has a chunky head which has leaf-like projections. The dark colored body is spotted with red and blue; the pectoral fins are tinged with yellow. This fish grows to a length of 8 inches. It is found off the southern Atlantic coast and sometimes as far north as Massachusetts.

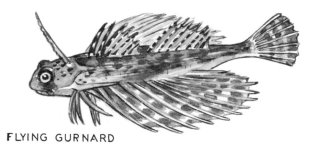

FLYING GURNARD

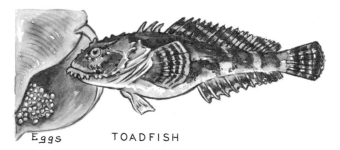

Eggs   TOADFISH

FLYING GURNARDS have winglike pectoral fins with which they are able to leap out of the water. Their ventral fins can be used like stilts for walking. The body is mottled brown and black, the pectoral fins are colorful. The Atlantic species grows to about a foot and the Pacific, a few inches longer.

The TOADFISH is mottled brownish on the back and has dark bands on the large pectoral and other fins. It grows to be a foot long and lives among weeds in shallow water along the Atlantic coast. The female lays eggs in cans, shells, or crevices and the male guards them. The toadfish can bite hard.

RED-NECKED   HORNED   GREBES   PIED-BILLED

DIVING BIRDS

Along all of our shores there are many kinds of water fowl. Among them are the diving birds. They have rather long necks and short legs. They live in the water most of the time since they are good swimmers and divers but poor walkers. They dive or dip under water to catch fish or pull up water plants.

GREBES

Grebes look like small ducks except for their pointed bills, very short tails, and short wings. They can fly, but they can take off only after running over the water. On land or ice they are almost helpless. They swim well and dive swiftly.

The male and female are alike in color and are usually lighter and duller in winter.

The RED-NECKED GREBE is greenish-black on the back, light gray on cheeks and throat, reddish-brown in front. It is 19 inches long.

The HORNED GREBE has a crested, greenish-black head with a buff patch, a reddish-brown front, and a grayish back. It is 14 inches long.

These two grebes are seen along both of our coasts in winter.

The PIED-BILLED GREBE, 13 inches long, is dark brownish on the back, light brown and white underneath; it has a black throat and a black ring on the bill. It is seen in fresh and brackish water along the eastern coast.

MERGANSERS

Mergansers are fishing ducks. They have narrow bills with toothed edges with which they catch fish. They are able to dive and swim under water. Mergansers are seen along both of our coasts in winter.

The COMMON OR AMERICAN MERGANSER is 25 inches long. The male has a dark green head, white lower neck, black back, and is black and white on the sides. The female has a crested, reddish-brown head, gray back, white undersides, and a white patch with black borders on the wings.

The RED-BREASTED MERGANSER is similar to the common in color, except that the male has a reddish-brown band on the breast. His head has a definite crest. He is 24 inches long.

The HOODED MERGANSER male has a large white crest on his black head. He is mostly black on the back, white underneath, and reddish-brown on the sides. The female is brownish on the back and white underneath. This merganser is 17½ inches long.

The common and hooded mergansers prefer fresh water. The red-breasted winters in salt water.

Female   Female   Female

Male   Male   Male

COMMON (AMERICAN)   RED-BREASTED   HOODED

MERGANSERS

MALLARDS   BLACK DUCK   BALDPATES

RIVER AND MARSH DUCKS

These ducks live mostly in shallow, fresh or brackish water. They usually nest and raise their young in Canada or the northern states. In fall and winter they migrate southward and are seen near the coast.

Ducks have broad, flat bills with which they pull up the water plants, pick up the mollusks, and catch the small fishes that they eat. When they feed on the bottom, they stand on their heads with their tails sticking up in the air. They also feed on land where they eat grasses, seeds, berries, and insects.

Ducks have strong wings and are able to fly at a good speed. The river ducks fly straight up when they take off from the water.

The MALLARD DUCK is common in ponds and marshes along both coasts as well as inland. It is 24 inches long. The male has a glossy green head and neck, a gray and brown back, a purple wing patch, and a black and white tail. The female is streaked light and dark brown, and she has a purple wing patch. The young and the male in summer, when he is molting, resemble the female.

The BLACK DUCK is the same size as the mallard and is often seen with it in the eastern states. Both the male and female are colored like the female mallard except that they are darker and do not have a white line along the purple wing patch.

The BLUE-WINGED TEAL is 16 inches long. The male has a gray and white head, a variegated brown body, and a blue shoulder. The female is light and dark brown with a blue shoulder. In winter these ducks are seen along the southeastern and Gulf coasts.

The GREEN-WINGED TEAL is 14 inches long. The male has a slightly crested head that is reddish-brown with green on the sides; he is grayish on the back, cream and black on the tail, and he has a green wing patch. The female is colored like a female mallard except for the green patch on her wing. In winter these teal are seen on our northeastern coast.

The BALDPATE or AMERICAN WIDGEON is about 21 inches long. The male is white on top and green on the sides of the head, reddish-brown on the breast, grayish-brown on the back; in flight a white patch shows on the front of the wing. The female is brownish with a light patch on the forewing. In winter baldpates are seen along both coasts. They feed mostly on water plants, dipping for them in shallow water and stealing them from better divers in deep water.

GREEN-WINGED TEALS   BLUE-WINGED TEALS

SCOTERS

SCAUP DUCKS

SEA DUCKS

These ducks are expert divers. They often go to the bottom in deep water to find the shellfish and plant roots that they eat. They have a lobe or web on the hind toe that helps them in swimming, but not in walking. Since they are clumsy on the land, they seldom go ashore. They sleep on the water. When they take off to fly they skitter across the water. The sea ducks nest mostly in Canada and the northern and western states. They are seen along our coasts in winter.

The COMMON SCOTER or SEA COOT is 17 to 21 inches long, the male being the larger. He is all black except for a yellow knob at the base of the bill. The female is grayish-brown with white on the cheeks and underneath. The SURF SCOTER is about the same size as the male sea coot. The male is black except for two white patches on his head and a yellow, orange, and black bill. The female is brownish. The WHITE-WINGED SCOTER is a little larger than the other two. The black male and the brown female both have a white wing patch. All three scoters are seen along both of our coasts in winter.

The GREATER SCAUP DUCK is 20 inches long. The male is black on the head, front, and tail, grayish on the back, and white underneath. The female is brownish with white at the base of her bill. Both sexes have short, wide, bluish bills. The LESSER SCAUP is like the larger one in color, but is more southern in its range. Flocks of scaup are often seen in bays and harbors along the eastern coast.

The CANVASBACK DUCK is 24 inches long. It has a sloping forehead and a long bill. The male is dark red on the head and neck, black around the lower neck, dark gray on the tail and very light gray on the back and sides. The female is duller in color. These ducks are seen along the East and Gulf coasts in winter. They like brackish water where there is plenty of eelgrass to eat.

The REDHEAD DUCK is 23 inches long. It has a high forehead and a rather short bill. The male has a reddish-brown head, a black neck and chest, and a gray back. The female is browner and duller in color. Redheads are seen along the eastern and California coasts in winter. They eat water plants, small fishes, and other water life.

CANVASBACKS

REDHEADS

WHISTLING SWAN   MUTE SWAN

SWANS

Swans are very large, white swimming birds with long, graceful necks. The male and female are alike in color and size. They mate for life. They nest on the ground near water, the wild swan in the far north, the domestic swan within its winter range. Both parents may take turns sitting on the two to eight eggs until they hatch in about forty days.

Swans eat plants and grain. They feed in shallow water by dipping their long necks under and sometimes tipping their tails up. They are awkward on land, but they are strong fliers.

The WILD or WHISTLING SWAN is seen in winter along the California coast and the Atlantic from Massachusetts southward. It is from 4 to 4½ feet long. Its bill is black with a yellow spot.

The DOMESTIC or MUTE SWAN is a tame bird brought from Europe or Asia. It now lives in a wild state on the eastern coast in the Long Island Sound area. It is nearly 5 feet long and has a yellow bill with a black knob at the base. Young swans have a brownish tinge and dusky bills.

GEESE

Geese are large water birds that have fairly long necks. They have short legs placed toward the middle of the body which enables them to walk better than swans or ducks. Geese often feed on land, eating grain and insects. In the water they eat eelgrass and the roots and seeds of water plants. They are strong fliers and travel from their nesting grounds in the far north to our southern coasts in winter. Male and female are alike in color.

The CANADA GOOSE is seen along both coasts in fall and winter. It grows to 3½ feet long and is black on the head and neck with a white chin strap, grayish-brown on the back. Flocks of migrating geese fly in V formation, often honking as they go.

BRANTS are smaller geese, about 2½ feet long. The AMERICAN BRANT, seen along the Atlantic Coast in winter, is black on the head, neck, and breast, with white streaks on each side of the neck; it is brownish-gray on the back, gray and white underneath. The BLACK BRANT of the Pacific coast is similar, but with more black underneath.

AMERICAN   BLACK
BRANTS   CANADA GOOSE

RING-BILLED   HERRING   LAUGHING   BLACK-BACKED

GULLS

GULLS AND TERNS

These are long-winged swimming birds. Gulls are large birds with slightly hooked bills. They are useful scavengers since they eat almost anything.

The HERRING GULL is common along the East Coast in winter and is also seen on the West Coast. It has a white body, gray back and black wing tips and grows to 26 inches long. The CALIFORNIA GULL is almost as large. It is white with a grayish back.

The RING-BILLED GULL is similar to the herring gull except that it is a little smaller and it has a black band around its greenish-yellow bill. It is seen along all of our coasts in winter.

The LAUGHING GULL is named after its call. It is 16 inches long and has a black head, white body and dark gray back. It nests along the eastern and southwestern coasts on sandy islands or marshes. In winter it is seen around the Gulf of Mexico.

The BLACK-BACKED GULL, with a length of 30 inches, is the largest of these gulls. It is white with a dark gray back. It is seen along our East Coast in winter.

Terns have straight, pointed bills and forked tails. When feeding they hover over the water then dive to catch fish and other sea life.

The CASPIAN TERN is 23 inches long and the ROYAL TERN is 20 inches. Both are white on the body and light bluish-gray on the back. They have a black crest on the head and a red or orange bill. Both birds are seen at nesting time along the southeastern coast; the Caspian is seen in winter on the West Coast.

The COMMON TERN nests on the East Coast and is seen on the West Coast during migration. It is 15 inches long and is white on the body, gray on the back, and black on the top of the head.

The LEAST TERN, 9 inches long, is similar to the common tern in color, except for its yellow bill and white forehead. It nests along the southern parts of both coasts.

The ARCTIC TERN, seen in migration along both coasts, nests in the Arctic and winters in the Antarctic. It is about 17 inches long and is light gray on the body, black on the top of the head.

COMMON   ROYAL   LEAST   ARCTIC

TERNS

BLACK-CROWNED NIGHT

HERONS

GREEN

HERONS

Herons usually have a long, slender look due to their long legs, long necks and bills. They wade in shallow water in lakes and marshes where they catch fish, insects, and small animals to eat. When they fly their rounded wings flap up and down. Herons nest in trees in the woods or among reeds in swamps.

The BLACK-CROWNED NIGHT HERON, 26 inches long, is black on the top of the head and back, gray on the wings, and white underneath. It usually folds its neck so that its head seems to rest on its shoulders. This heron is seen along tidal creeks, marshes, and ponds on the East Coast throughout the year and in California in winter.

The GREEN HERON is 18 inches long. It is dark greenish on the top of the head and back, reddish-brown on the back of the neck, white with dark streaks on the front. Its neck may either be stretched up or folded against its shoulders. Young birds are streaked light and dark brown. This heron is seen at the edge of rivers and marshes along our southern and eastern coasts.

The GREAT BLUE HERON stands 4 feet tall as it waits for its prey along the shore of fresh or salt water. It is bluish-gray and has a white crown bordered with long black feathers. These large herons are seen in summer along both coasts, and in winter along the southern parts of the East Coast.

The COMMON OR AMERICAN EGRET, 41 inches long, is a little smaller than the blue heron. This egret is white, and it has a train of long plumes on its back in the breeding season. It has a yellow bill, black legs and feet. The SNOWY EGRET is smaller, 24 inches long. It has a black bill, black legs, and yellow feet. At breeding time it has a crest of plumes on its head and white plumes on its back. Both egrets are seen along our southern coasts at nesting time and sometimes in the northeast in summer.

GREAT
BLUE
HERON

SNOWY
EGRETS   COMMON

LEAST
Male   BITTERNS   Female

VIRGINIA   SORA
RAILS

BITTERNS AND RAILS

Bitterns belong to the heron family. They live in fresh-water or salt marshes where they hide among the tall grasses. Their nest is a platform of plant stems built among cattails or reeds. Their food consists of small marsh animals and insects.

The AMERICAN BITTERN is 24 inches or longer. Its back is light and dark brown speckled with black and white; it is white on the chin, light yellowish with dark streaks on the front. It has a yellow and brown bill and greenish-yellow legs. When it stands among the marsh grasses with its head pointed up it looks like part of the landscape.

The LEAST BITTERN is from 11 to 14 inches long. The male is greenish-black on the top of the head, back, and tail, and the female is brownish. Both are reddish-brown on the wings and yellow-brown underneath with dark streaks.

Both kinds of bitterns nest along both of our coasts and inland. Most winter in the southern states although some American bitterns stay farther north.

Rails are stocky, henlike birds with big feet; some have long, others, short bills. They live in marshes where they eat snails, insects, small crustaceans, seeds, and water plants.

The VIRGINIA RAIL is 10 or 11 inches long. It is olive-brown with dark streaks on the back, gray on the side of the head, white on the chin, reddish-brown on the front, gray and white underneath.

The SORA RAIL is a small, plump bird, only 9 inches long. It is olive brown with light and dark markings on the back, black around the bill, gray on the front, brownish with white bars underneath.

Virginia and sora rails usually nest in fresh water marshes, but they are seen along the western and southeastern coasts in the winter.

The CLAPPER RAIL nests in salt marshes in the middle part of our eastern coast and spends the winter there or farther south. It is about 16 inches long. On the back it is brownish-gray with darker streaks; on the throat, white; underneath, grayish with white bands. In winter it is darker.

AMERICAN
BITTERNS

CLAPPER
RAIL

PLOVERS

PLOVERS

Plovers are the rather small brown and white or black and white birds seen on beaches and in fields. Male and female are colored alike. Their legs are not very long, and they have medium to short bills.

The BLACK-BELLIED PLOVER, about 13 inches long, is the largest. It is black and white on the back, white along the side of the head and neck, black underneath. In winter it is more grayish.

The RINGED or SEMI-PALMATED PLOVER, 6 to 8 inches long, is brown on the back, white underneath. It has one ring of black around its neck. These plovers sleep on beaches and feed at the edge of the water.

The black-bellied and the ringed plovers nest in the far north. They are seen along both coasts during migration and in the southern states in winter.

The KILLDEER, named after its call, is a little larger than the ringed plover and is similar in color except that it has two black bands around its neck. This plover nests in fields or on beaches near all of our coasts. It may raise two families in a season.

TURNSTONES AND OYSTERCATCHERS

The turnstone receives its name from its habit of sticking its bill under stones and turning them over to find worms, insects, or small sea animals to eat.

The RUDDY TURNSTONE is 9 inches long. The male is black and white with reddish-brown markings on the back. The female is duller. Both birds are gray and brown instead of black in the winter. They nest in the far north, but they are seen along our coasts during migration, and winter in the southern parts. The BLACK-HEADED TURNSTONE, seen in winter on our western coast, is a little smaller. It is black on the head, neck, and chest; white underneath.

OYSTERCATCHERS are so named because they feed on oysters and other mollusks. They open them by inserting their strong bills between the shells. The common OYSTERCATCHER is 21 inches long and is black on the head, brown on the back, and white underneath. It lives along our southern coasts where it nests in a hollow in the sand. The BLACK OYSTER-CATCHER of the West Coast is a little smaller. It is black and brownish.

RUDDY BLACK-HEADED
TURNSTONES

BLACK COMMON
OYSTERCATCHERS

LEAST   SEMI-PALMATED   SPOTTED

SANDPIPERS

SANDPIPERS

Sandpipers are small wading birds that run along the shore on slender legs. With their long bills they dig in the sand or search in grasses, among stones, or at the edge of the water for worms, mollusks, small crustaceans, insects, and other small animal food to eat. Sandpipers are seen along our shores during migration, and they winter in the south. Male and female are usually alike in color. In winter they are duller and paler.

The LEAST SANDPIPER is only 6 inches long. It is grayish-brown with darker markings on its back, white underneath, light brown with dark spots on the breast. Flocks of these little sandpipers are seen on beaches and marshes along both of our coasts.

The SEMI-PALMATED SANDPIPER is about the same size as the least, but it has a thicker bill. It is brownish on the back, white underneath with dark spots on the breast. These sandpipers are seen on the East Coast running along the beach at the edge of the waves. The WESTERN SANDPIPER, which is seen in the southeastern states in winter, is similar.

The SPOTTED SANDPIPER is seen all across our country near ponds and streams in summer, and along our southern coasts in winter. It is 7 or 8 inches long and is brown on the back, white underneath with round dark spots. When it walks it bobs its tail up and down. It can dive and swim under water if necessary.

The PURPLE SANDPIPER is seen on rocky shores along our northeastern coast in winter. It is a stocky bird from 8 to 9½ inches long. It is dark gray on the back and breast, white underneath, and its short legs are yellow.

The DUNLIN or RED-BACKED SANDPIPER is 8 or 9 inches long. It is seen along our western and southeastern coasts in winter, when it is dark grayish on the back, light gray underneath.

The PECTORAL SANDPIPER is seen on mud flats and marshes along the Atlantic and southern California coasts in the fall. It is about 9 inches long and is dark brown on the back, white underneath, light brown with dark streaks on the breast.

The SANDERLING is common in winter along both coasts except in the northern parts. It is about 8 inches long and is the lightest colored of the small sandpipers. In winter it is pale gray on the back and white underneath. Flocks of sanderlings run along beaches at the edge of the waves where they find small animal life and algae to eat.

PURPLE   RED-BACKED or DUNLIN   PECTORAL   SANDERLING

SANDPIPERS

KNOT   DOWITCHER

LESSER   GREATER
YELLOWLEGS

WADING BIRDS

The KNOT is a chunky bird, about 10 inches long, In summer it is grayish-brown on the back and reddish on the breast. In winter it is mostly gray on the back, white underneath with dark markings on breast and sides. Flocks of knots are seen on the sandy shores of our East Coast in spring and fall.

DOWITCHERS are about 12 inches long. They are reddish-brown on the back and breast in summer (grayish in winter), white on the tail and rump. One kind has a 2½ inch long bill, the other kind has a longer bill. Dowitchers are seen along both coasts in migration and in the south in winter.

YELLOWLEGS are gray and brown on the back, white underneath with gray spots on the breast and neck. They have long bills and long, slender, yellow legs. The GREATER YELLOWLEGS is 15 inches long and is seen in winter along our southern coasts. The LESSER YELLOWLEGS is 11 inches long and is seen along the East Coast in fall and the south in winter.

The WILLET is 16 inches long, grayish with darker markings and white on the tail; large white wing patches show in flight. Willets nest in fresh or salt water marshes along the East Coast. The western one is similar but a little larger.

CURLEWS have long, curved bills. They are reddish-brown with light and dark markings on the back, lighter underneath. The LONG-BILLED CURLEW, 26 inches long, is seen along our West Coast and in the southeast in winter. The HUDSONIAN CURLEW, or WHIMBREL, 18 inches long, is seen along both coasts during migration.

GODWITS have long, slightly upcurved bills. The HUDSONIAN GODWIT, which is seen along the Atlantic coast in the fall, is 16 inches long. It is dark brown with lighter marking on the back and reddish-brown underneath in summer. In the winter it is grayish with a white spot above the tail. The MARBLED GODWIT is seen on both coasts during migration and in the southeastern states in winter. It is 21 inches long and is reddish-brown with light and dark markings on the back, lighter underneath.

WILLET   WHIMBREL or HUDSONIAN   LONG-BILLED   CURLEWS   HUDSONIAN   MARBLED   GODWITS

MORE TO READ

BIRDS

American Water and Game Birds, Rand (Dutton)
Audubon Water Bird Guide, The, Pough (Doubleday)
Birds, Zim and Gabrielson (Golden Press)
Birds of America, Pearson, Editor (Garden City)
Birds of the Ocean, Alexander (Putnam)
Field Guide to the Birds, Eastern Land and Water Birds, The, Peterson (Houghton)
Field Guide to Western Birds, A, Peterson (Houghton)
Florida Bird Life, Sprunt (Coward-McCann)
Pocket Guide to the Birds, The, Cruickshank (Dodd)
Sea-birds, Fisher and Lockley (Houghton)
Water Birds of the Pacific States, Hoffman (Houghton)

FISHES

Book of Fishes, The (National Geographic)
Common Ocean Fishes of the California Coast, Roedel (State of California Department of Fish and Game, Fish Bulletin No. 91)
Field Book of Marine Fishes of the Atlantic Coast, Breder (Putnam)
Fishes, Zim and Shoemaker (Golden Press)
Life Story of the Fish, The, Curtis (Harcourt Brace)
North American Games Fishes, La Monte (Doubleday)

FLOWERS, TREES, AND SHRUBS

Beginner's Guide to Wild Flowers, Hausman (Putnam)
Field Book of American Trees and Shrubs, Mathews (Putnam)
Field Book of Western Wild Flowers, Armstrong (Putnam)
Field Guide to the Wildflowers of the Northeastern and Central States, McKenny and Peterson (Houghton)
Flowers, Zim and Martin (Golden Press)

SEAWEEDS

How to Know the Seaweeds, Dawson (W. C. Brown Co.)
Seaweeds at Ebb Tide, Guberlet (University of Washington Press)

SHELLS

American Seashells, Abbott (D. Van Nostrand)
Book of Sea Shells, The, Bevans (Doubleday)
Field Guide to Shells of the Pacific Coast and Hawaii, A, Morris (Houghton)
Field Guide to the Shells of Our Atlantic and Gulf Coasts, A, Morris (Houghton)
My Hobby is Collecting Seashells and Coral, Dudley (Childrens Press)
Sea Shells of the World, Abbott (Golden Press)
Sea Treasure, Johnstone (Houghton)
Shell Collector's Handbook, Verill (Putnam)

GENERAL

Edge of the Sea, The, Carson (Houghton)
Fieldbook of Natural History, Palmer (McGraw-Hill)
Fieldbook of Seashore Life, Miner (Putnam)
Golden Book of Science, Morris Parker (Golden Press)
Hammond's Nature Atlas of America, Jordan (Doubleday)
Pagoo, Holling (Houghton)
Sea and Shore, Hylander (Macmillan)
Seashore Animals of the Pacific Coast, Johnson and Snook (Macmillan)
Seashores, Zim and Ingle (Golden Press)
Wonderful World of the Seashore, The, Gaul (Appleton)
Wonders of the Seashore, Berrill (Dodd)
Zoology, Burnett, Fisher, and Zim (Golden Press)

MAGAZINES

Audubon Magazine, National Audubon Society, New York
Junior Natural History, American Museum of Natural History, New York
National Wildlife, National Wildlife Federation, Washington
Nature Magazine, American Nature Association, Washington